Promise only what you can deliver.

Then deliver more than you promise.

~Author Unknown

ONE PROMISE KEPT

The case that made a cop,
and others that almost broke him

By Steve Webster
With Trevor Maxwell

Cover art by Chelée Ross and Sam Howe.
Logo by Jason Young
Article headlines courtesy of the Portland Press Herald.

Printed at Brown Fox Printing, Scarborough, ME

This logo was designed by Jason Young and it represents who I am and what I believe in. The rings represent committment, the cross stands for sacrifice, and the anchor is a symbol of hope. Finally, the crane symbolizes honor, which to many of us is more than just a word.

Any opinions or views expressed in this book are mine alone and not those of any local, state, or federal entity.

Prologue

I am just like you in so many ways. I sweat, I feel pain, and I bleed. I am often forced to hide my emotions and ignore the pain, so I can get my job done and get through the day.

I am a police officer and I love my job and hate my job. I appreciate all that I have because I see so many people who have nothing.

Some officers see more death, degradation, and heartache in one shift than you will experience in a lifetime. They don't complain because it comes with the job. The badge we wear doesn't stand for power, it is a shield. We do our best to help those who need it, and shield those who can't protect themselves.

You are about to get a glimpse into my world. Its not always pretty, the cases don't get wrapped up in an hour as they do on tv, and the decisions we are forced to make in an instant can be scrutinized for years.

I have had the dreadful taste of death in my mouth and seen horrors that keep me up at night. I'm not complaining, I'm explaining.

I am just like you in so many ways, yet so different in others. What you consider catastrophic I may consider an inconvenience. I see the world though unfiltered eyes. I am no better or worse than you; just different. I want you to better understand who I am, and at the same time gain a better understanding of myself.

I truly believe that destination is secondary to the journey. You are about to stand beside me as I take a look back at mine.

Acknowledgments

Steve -

I would like to thank my family for their support and understanding during the long process of writing, re-writing, and re-writing this book. I'm sure they understood that I had to get it out. This book wouldn't have been possible without the friendship, keen insight, and honest feedback from some people that I hold in high regard. Angie Cannon shared her intelligence, Alicia Cummings shared her ideas, and Ray and Dee Dee Richardson let me borrow a bit of both. Joe Loughlin was kind enough to share his insight. Trevor, I will always consider myself a storyteller, and you are the true writer. I couldn't have done this without you. Your future is looking bright. To my MDEA buddies, you folks rock, especially Larry Tiita. I took a chance by having two college students do the cover art and they came through with flying colors. Chelée Ross and Sam Howe, you are this country's future and for that I am grateful.

Finally, I would be remiss if I didn't thank all of those I have served with side by side over the course of my career. You are some of the finest men and women in the world, and you have taught me, enlightened me, and encouraged me to push the envelope just a bit more. It has been quite a ride because of you. Stay safe and be well.

Trevor -

To my wife Sarah and my daughters, Sage and Elsie, thanks for encouraging me to work on this project and for helping me find the time to make it happen. To Steve, thanks for trusting me with your stories and your voice. You are a natural storyteller; all I did was dress it up a little. Most of all, thanks for being a friend.

Table of Contents

Chapter 1

The robbery

The parking lot at the apartment complex was almost empty. No crime scene tape, no media, no supervisor barking orders.

As I pulled my unmarked police cruiser into the lot, I was hopeful this was just another bogus robbery complaint. Maybe I'd get to end my shift early and finally get out to the fishing hole for some peace and quiet.

A patrol officer met me at the door of apartment 101 at the Olde English Village building in South Portland. One look inside and I realized my afternoon was definitely not going to involve a fishing rod and a six-pack.

The place was trashed. Clothing scattered everywhere. Broken furniture. It was messier than the first apartment I rented back when I was single. I threw out the obligatory *holy shit* as I walked room to room through the wreckage. Either someone had gone into a rage, or they came here looking for something and they weren't going to stop until they found it.

A small Buddha statue sat near the smashed television, and from the smell of the apartment, someone had recently cooked Asian food. A photograph of an attractive Asian woman still hung, as if by some miracle, on the wall.

I gathered my thoughts and called my supervisor, expecting him to send some help.

"So you're all set?" he said.

I wasn't sure if he was asking me or telling me.

By that point in my career with the South Portland Police Department, I was pretty confident. In my 10 years assigned to patrol, I had seen a lot of crime scenes. But I had only been a detective for about a year and a half, and the Detective Bureau is a whole different ballgame from patrol.

"Yep, all set," I told him.

I could never admit to my boss that I didn't know where to start. I've always felt that if you have no idea what you're doing, act like you know anyway.

Our police dispatcher didn't have much information, except for a telephone call from a nail salon near the Maine Mall. The caller said he owned the salon, and that his apartment across the street had just been robbed. His 7-year-old daughter and his 10-year-old niece were the only ones home when it happened.

I got the call about halfway into my shift, which was 1 to 9 p.m. on that day, June 23, 1998.

On the short drive from headquarters to the apartment, I thought about what I would need to bring inside and who I would need to contact. I've always had a habit of daydreaming, but I think it's a good habit.

Before I became a detective, when I was still in uniform as a patrol officer, I would sit in my cruiser and run scenarios through my head: A traffic stop gone bad, a drunk wanting to kick my ass, even someone pulling a gun on me. Each time, I would imagine how I would react, how I would survive, how I would get home safe to my family.

Standing in the middle of the wrecked apartment, I took a deep breath and started doing what I get paid to do. I was careful not to disturb anything because we might be able to get some fingerprints. I called for an evidence technician to process the scene and to take photographs.

There was a small bedroom at the back of the apartment. I noticed a cord from a video game machine lying on the bottom mattress on a set of bunk beds. There was also a loose strap that appeared to have been ripped off a purse. The patrol officer told me a group of men had tied the little girls up while they ransacked the place. The girls and their families were at the nail salon across the street.

My blood ran hot. Who could be cruel enough to go into an apartment, tie up two little girls and do that kind of damage? What would my reaction have been if the victims were my own kids? It wasn't a pleasant thought.

Workers at the salon were still serving customers in small booths set up on each side of the building. Even as work was being done, though, the place was quiet. I felt the eyes on me as one of the employees led me to a small room at the back of the salon. I guessed it was the break room. Squeezed into the room were some chairs, a couch and a television. A few adults were talking and two young Asian girls sat on the floor watching cartoons.

I knelt down.

"My name is Steve. I'm a policeman, and I'm going to find out who did this to you," I said.

"Can you tell me your names?"

Alex was the 7-year-old. Her parents, Don and Monica Tran, owned the salon.

Julie, the 10-year-old, was Alex's cousin. She and her mother had just moved to Maine about a week earlier, and they were staying with the Tran family in the apartment.

It was clear that Alex was not an ordinary 7-year-old. Instead of looking away, she looked straight at me. She was the cutest little girl with long, jet black hair and big brown eyes.

Alex had the pained expression of a child who had just been hurt, but she was not crying. There was something strong about her, something that told me she had not lost her pride. I was struck right away by her maturity. If that were me and someone had just stuck a gun to my head, I'd probably be curled up in a corner sucking my thumb. But here was little Alex, looking right at me and ready to answer my questions.

Her mother was on the couch. I recognized her as the woman in the photograph at the apartment.

Monica Tran was clearly upset about what had happened to her daughter, yet at the same time I got the impression that I wasn't supposed to know she was upset. She spoke softly and said very little. It didn't bother me, but I didn't understand why she was acting that way.

Don Tran was easier to read. The look of anger on his face said it all. I had a pretty good idea what he would have done to those cowards that tied up his daughter. Don was older than his wife. I was impressed by the large Buddha hanging around his neck and the collection of gold jewelry he was wearing.

For the next half-hour, I asked Alex and Julie questions about what had happened.

The girls had been at the salon earlier that afternoon. Around 3 o'clock they decided to go back to the apartment to have a snack and watch some television. The Olde English Village apartment building could be seen from the front windows of the salon. A few minutes after they got there, Alex and Julie heard a knock at the apartment door. They figured it was a friend or neighbor. In order to get into the apartment building, you either had to have a key or someone needed to buzz you in.

A male voice asked if Kevin was home. Kevin was Monica Tran's brother. He lived at the apartment and was working at the nail salon that afternoon. Julie opened the door just enough to see who was there. That was all it took.

Two men pushed the door open and took the girls into their bedroom. They used the video game cord and the strap from a purse to bind the girls' arms and feet. One of the men, the girls said, was Vietnamese. He was chubby, with tattoos on his hand. He kept asking Alex, *"Where's the money? Where's the money?"*

The other guy pointed a gun at Alex's head. He threatened to shoot if she wouldn't answer. Begging for her life, Alex kept telling them the truth. She didn't know about any money.

Two more men came into the apartment. They were talking to each other and looking everywhere. For the girls, time seemed to pass in slow motion.

When the men realized that they weren't going to find what they came for, they got really angry. They toppled the furniture, threw stuff around and even tossed the telephone into the toilet bowl. They ripped the gold necklaces from the necks of Alex and Julie. One of the men then put towels in their mouths and used duct tape to hold the gags in place.

Finally the men left. There was silence. The girls struggled and managed to get free of the cord and the strap, and they removed the gags from their mouths. Terrified, the girls didn't dare to leave the apartment because they thought the men might still be outside, and they couldn't call over to the salon because the phone was ruined.

When an hour had passed and the girls had not returned, Kevin was worried. He walked from the salon over to the apartment to check on them.

As the girls told me about the robbery, I nodded and reassured them calmly. These girls were extremely lucky. I had heard stories such as this turning deadly.

Alex and Julie both provided details of their attackers that I wouldn't even expect to get from adults. They described each of the four Asian men, from approximate ages to hairstyles, height, weight and tattoos. They even remembered that one of the men, whom they described as the oldest of the group, had a distinctive mole on the side of his face.

I thanked them for their patience and told them how brave they were, and that I would probably be speaking with them soon.

Alex looked straight at me again with her wide, dark eyes.

"Are you going to catch them?" she said.

I made the promise without hesitation or even a hint of uncertainty. Yes, I told Alex. I'm going to catch those men so they can't do this to anyone else.

That night, as I drove home to tuck my own kids in bed, my mind kept going back to that moment, and to the single thought that would stick with me for the months to come.

Don't let her down.

Chapter Two

Maine, Germany and back again

I gave up the dream of playing shortstop for the Red Sox during my sophomore year in high school, when I quit sports.

That was 1980, the year my parents told me that I had to keep up my grades if I wanted to work. It was all about need for me; I needed a job if I wanted to drive, and my parents weren't going to pay the insurance bill for me.

The thought of hitting the open road in the 1974 Plymouth Valiant that was sitting in the driveway was just too tempting.

My first job was at Friendly's Ice Cream shop, but it wasn't for me so I took a job at a shoe manufacturer, where my uncle worked. That suited me much better, and I worked there part-time during the school year and full-time in the summers.

I earned enough money to pay for car insurance, gas and other expenses, and my dad rewarded me by giving me the Valiant.

Ours was a working class family. My dad was a firefighter and a commercial painter, and my mom was one of the fastest typists I have ever seen. They raised me and my sister, who is 18 months older than I am, in the city of Westbrook, which borders both Portland and South Portland.

Today, Westbrook is struggling like so many other cities in New England that are making the transition from mill town to something else. But in the days of my childhood, the city was still defined by its largest employer, the huge paper mill at the center of town. It may have smelled bad to people from away, but to most people from Westbrook, it was the smell of jobs and money. People punched the clock and played in baseball or softball leagues after work and on the weekends.

Growing up in Westbrook wasn't too bad for me. I brought home average grades and spent most of my free time playing sports with the kids in our neighborhood.

Jim Fahey was my best friend growing up, and he lived right down the street. Like my dad, Jim's dad also was a firefighter. We spent our summers pretending to be Dwight Evans and Jim Rice, and our winters on the frozen ponds, imaginary Bobby Orrs. Jim and I were pretty much inseparable, and complimented each other well. He was quite sociable and well liked by the girls, and I wasn't opposed to tagging along.

By senior year in high school, my long range goal was simple: graduate. I managed to scrape by with Cs and an occasional B, which kept my parents happy. I had no idea what I wanted to do once I got that diploma in my hand, but I didn't see college as an option. Hell, I didn't even like high school, so I had little desire to apply to Harvard or Yale. Why pay for something that I didn't enjoy?

As most of my classmates were making plans for college or lining up jobs, I enlisted in the Army at the age of 17. My parents had to sign a special waiver. I can't say my reasons were great, but I figured a change of scenery would do me good. I had watched all those John Wayne movies when I was growing up, and was always fascinated with the scenes depicting the battlefields of World War II.

In June of 1983 I got my diploma, 24 hours to celebrate, and a plane ticket to Philadelphia. From there, I got on a bus destined for a place in New Jersey that I later learned was affectionately called the asshole of the Army, Fort Dix.

All of us were raw recruits on that green bus. I scanned my competition during the drive and realized that I was probably the only guy from Maine, sitting amongst mostly black guys who I assumed had just come off the streets of the inner city. Maybe it was the fear, maybe it was the anxiety of being plucked out of my familiar surroundings, but something was making my blood pump faster, and I liked the rush.

I arrived at Fort Dix as a shy, immature kid. As the weeks flew by, I found myself becoming vocal out of necessity. I didn't want to get stomped on in my new environment. It was not a difficult adjustment. Showering with 50 other guys tends to bring you out of your shell in a hurry.

With my newfound voice came newfound confidence. The Army was throwing obstacles in front of me and I was going over them or through them, whatever it took. Eight weeks of non-stop, hunger riddled, sleep-deprived training made me one cocky bastard. I admit that my energy was tough to harness, and I had a chip on my shoulder, but for the first time in my life I felt that I had earned it.

My dad had signed the form allowing me to enlist, but he also made me promise to learn a trade while serving my country. So for several weeks after basic training ended, I remained at Fort Dix to be trained as a mechanic.

One day is all it took for me to realize that I had made a big mistake. I could shoot an M-16, read a compass, march all day without complaint, but I was no mechanic. To this day, ask me to fix anything mechanical, and I'm screwed.

Somehow I managed to complete the training even though I was probably the worst mechanic that Uncle Sam had ever seen. I couldn't wait to leave Fort Dix, and didn't really care where they sent me.

My drill instructor, Sergeant Grant, was a very large black gentleman who intimidated the shit out of me. I'm sure that deep down inside he was a great guy, but unfortunately I never saw that side of him. Sergeant Grant was kind enough to hand me a form one day that he described as a dream sheet. It asked me where I would like to serve once I departed lovely Fort Dix. If my memory serves me well, I requested a direct flight to Hawaii.

Someone got confused, or perhaps my penmanship was messy, because when my orders came down I was headed for Germany. No warm sandy beaches there, but what the hell.

A group of about 100 soldiers sat in the processing center in Frankfurt, waiting to hear what bases we would be assigned to.

In the afternoon, a short guy with blond hair came in and spoke to us. He said he was recruiting a few good men to join his unit. It was a volunteer assignment. You could volunteer to go, but if it didn't work out, the unit could voluntarily get rid of you. My hand was in the air within seconds.

I had plenty of time to think during the hour-long drive to our destination. Blondie wasn't talking, and neither was the only other guy from our group who had fallen for this guy's spiel. I thought I made another mistake. Why would only two out of 100 people get into that Jeep?

The front entrance to the small airbase at Gieblestadt was secured by towering metal gates, which looked ominous as we approached. Inside, we were introduced to the First Sergeant who was sitting in his office. The conversation was brief. Ten seconds brief. He said welcome and off we went with Blondie. He brought us to a small equipment room and handed us our rucksacks. We were about to be indoctrinated into the 3rd Infantry Division Long Range Reconnaissance Unit.

First order of business was a speed march that kicked my ass, but I refused to quit. Blondie drove the Jeep around the seldom used airfield, while we followed closely behind on foot, weighed down by about 80 pounds of gear. After passing the test, we were quickly accepted by the other members of the unit.

I had finally found my home in the Army. Over the next two years I would become entwined with some of the finest soldiers who have ever worn Army green. Soldiers who taught me lessons I carry with me to this day about teamwork, trust and loyalty.

The entire unit, which answered directly to the commander of the 3rd Infantry Division, consisted of about 30 people. Our mission was similar to that of the Ranger Division or Special Forces. But while they wanted to be seen, we couldn't be. We trained to be dropped miles behind enemy lines and to let the good guys know what was coming. This was in case war broke out in Europe. There was still an East and West Germany at the time, and the tension was high. The toppling of the Berlin Wall, and a unified Germany, remained several years away.

Like most others in the unit, I worked hard and played harder. We would spend days at a time training deep in the woods of various locations in Europe, and when we returned to our quarters we found ways to unwind. To the best of my recollection, the members of our unit drank more than their fair share of alcohol, myself included.

Germany went so well for me, it was the biggest reason why I did not stay in the Army.

When it came time for reenlistment, I had a tough decision to make. I knew that if I reenlisted, I'd probably become a career soldier. In some ways that was appealing, but the vision I kep having was that I would be stuck for years in some mechanized infantry unit in Oklahoma. Ultimately, I just couldn't stand the idea of going backwards like that. So I decided to go home.

The next big decision, of course, was what to do with the rest of my life. The answer actually came to me shortly before I came back to Maine. That same First Sergeant, the one who had barely spoken to me upon my arrival at Gieblestadt, let me read one of his books one day. I was headed to the reading room, sometimes known as the toilet, and the book I carried was a textbook. Basics of Criminal Justice. I read for a few minutes and some of the information clicked in my mind. Law enforcement sounded like an interesting career, and my Army background made me a perfect candidate.

A few phone calls later, I was registered for classes at a technical college in South Portland. My next big move. It was that simple.

I arrived back in Maine with $12 in my pocket, two fresh tattoos, and a rocking stereo system. I also had a new appreciation for some words that had been in my vocabulary for a long time, but I had never understood.

Teamwork was clearly defined by those I served with in Germany. It was all about the mission and taking care of each other. My initiation into the philosophy of leadership came from Capt. John Provost, a quiet man who led from the front. He never asked us to do anything that he wasn't willing and able to do himself.

I also returned to the states with vivid and fond memories of brutal runs that we completed as a unit. Capt. Provost didn't watch us. He led the way. I still remember the burning lungs, the pain in my knees and heels, and all I could think about was how much worse it would hurt if I let him and the team down. As I headed home, I knew that was the kind of leader I wanted to be.

Chapter Three

Building the case

As I walked through the salon looking for Don or Monica Tran, I noticed the same harsh chemical smell from the day before.

I returned to the salon as soon as possible because I wanted to show them that I would spend every available minute working on this case.

Monica sat in a chair, painting a woman's nails, and she managed a quick smile when she saw me. Then she told me she would get her husband, who was cleaning the apartment across the street. I waited, expecting to have a conversation with Monica. I couldn't understand why she basically ignored me and kept painting nails.

It was the first time that I had worked with victims who were from Southeast Asia, and whose backgrounds were so different from my own. I felt lost.

That morning, before going to the salon, I made some phone calls. I wanted to talk to some detectives in larger cities, people who had day-to-day contact with Asians from all different countries and cultures. One seasoned investigator gave me a piece of advice. If I ever developed suspects, which he doubted, he suggested the way to approach an interview. Southeast Asian suspects seldom talk to police in general, he said, and if they do they are not easily bluffed. The investigator told me to throw all of the evidence at the suspect, and if he feels that he is caught red-handed, there's a good chance he'll confess. But if the suspect thinks you're bluffing and that you're full of shit, he'll clam up.

Don walked into the salon. When Alex saw the two of us talking, she walked out of the break room where she had been watching television.

Shy is not a word I would use to describe Alex. She had an unusual confidence for a second-grader. She came right up to me and once again looked me in the eyes. I joked around with her for a few minutes. As much as I needed the support of her parents, I needed Alex's trust even more.

She wore stunning gold jewelry around her neck and wrists. The men had ripped her old jewelry from her during the robbery, and Don had gone out that morning to buy her new pieces. I asked him if the jewelry was real – meaning authentic gold, far better than the chain I had dangling around my own neck. Don told me that Asians don't buy cheap jewelry, and that he preferred 18 or 24 carat gold. Another lesson learned.

Don and I went outside, and for the next two hours or so we talked. I got his thoughts about the robbery, asked him about anyone who might want revenge against him, and all the while I absorbed everything he was telling me about his family and how they landed in Maine.

Don had grown up in Vietnam and Monica was from neighboring Cambodia. Both of their families had experienced absolute horror during wars in their countries, and they had come to the U.S. to escape the violence.

The couple met in 1989, when their families were living in Atlanta. Don was much older, and they married when Monica was still a teenager. The Trans moved from Atlanta to North Carolina because the crime rate was lower. A friend then suggested they move to Maine because there weren't many nail salons here. Don and Monica decided Maine would be a nice place to open a salon and raise their children.

Somebody knew, or at least thought, the Trans had money. It was true that their business was doing well, but Don certainly was not rich. Don did not know of any enemies and the family was well liked in the community. I asked him if he had any problems with his employees. Again, he told me that he did not.

Then I asked him if any employees had left recently. Most of the workers hired by the Trans worked long enough to make some money and move on; that's why Don and Monica end up working so many hours themselves.

A worker named Kieu (pronounced Q) had left the salon a few weeks before the robbery. Kieu had come from North Carolina and he worked for the Trans for a few months. Kieu had struck up a relationship with Paula, Monica's sister-in-law. Paula also worked at the salon. Her husband, Monica Tran's brother, was in prison.

Kieu and Paula had quite the romance going, and they had decided to return to North Carolina and open a nail salon there. Don supported the idea, and he even gave them some money to help them get started.

Could Kieu have been involved in the robbery, I asked Don.

"No," he said without a flicker of doubt. "I don't think so."

During our talk outside the salon, Don mentioned a couple of local teenage girls who had become friendly with some of his employees. Just within the past couple of days, the girls had taken a bus to North Carolina to visit Kieu, Paula and her younger brother, who was the same age as the girls. They had stopped by the salon to pick up some things for Kieu before leaving.

I decided to pay a visit to the girls' mother, who lived only a few minutes away.

The house was a large split level in a nice neighborhood in Scarborough, a suburban town that borders South Portland. I rang the doorbell and a woman hollered down at me from a window, asking what I wanted. I explained as politely as I could that I was a police officer, and I needed to speak with her.

The Chevy Camaro I was driving certainly didn't look like a police car, and I have to admit that my attire was less than an Armani suit. My personal style usually consists of jeans, a t-shirt and a sport coat thrown on top to convince people that I'm dressed up.

She wasn't buying the Miami Vice look, and she actually called the cops on me. This was going well.

One of our dispatchers convinced her that I was indeed a South Portland police officer. Mary calmed down, but she was a fast and loud talker. She had heard about the robbery on the news, but Mary couldn't understand why I was looking for her daughters. I tried to explain the situation without telling her too much.

Mary confirmed that her daughters, 16-year-old Jessica and 13-year-old Alicia, had met Paula and Kieu while getting their nails done, and they had become friends. Mary let her daughters take a bus to North Carolina to visit them and Paula's little brother, who they knew as "T". I was questioning Mary's judgment already and I had only been in her house less than 10 minutes.

I stressed to Mary that I wanted to talk to the girls because I needed to follow up on any and every suspicion or lead that I had.

Within a few minutes I was on the phone with Jessica in North Carolina. She answered my questions, but the only problem was she was being less than pleasant. I have a hard time listening to a 16-year-old swearing at me constantly and telling me where I can go.

Alicia was kind enough to get on the phone before I hung up, and she too wished me a nice day in her own special way.

First impressions mean a lot, and I didn't like these girls.

Once again, politely, I suggested that Mary get the girls home as soon as possible. Despite the fact that I didn't think Kieu or Paula had anything to do with the robbery, it was too early to rule anyone out. What I didn't tell her was that I wanted Jessica and Alicia back in Maine so I could meet with them face to face and give them a friendly attitude adjustment.

Over the course of the next few days, I spoke with the girls on the phone. They not only refused to come home, they continued to tell me what I should do with myself in my spare time. Man were they pleasant.

I talked to Kieu once on the phone. He was cordial and agreeable. He also told the girls to go home, but they threatened to run away if he put them on a bus. What a shame that would have been.

For the first couple weeks after the robbery, I went back to the salon almost every day. I would sit outside and talk with Don. Alex would always see us and run up with a big smile and a hug.

I chatted with her about her new jewelry and how she felt about starting second grade in the fall.

One day I promised her to take her for ice cream at the end of the week. Sure enough, when I showed up to speak with Don, Alex reminded me of what I said. Kids don't forget, so out we went.

I needed Alex to like and trust me, because I knew that at some point she might have to pick suspects out of a lineup, or even testify at a trial. But it was deeper than that for me. I wanted her to be all right. Not the next week or the next month, but 20 years down the road. I wanted her to know that what happened to her was not acceptable, and there were people like me whose job it is to protect her and punish those men for what they did.

Every now and then you become consumed with a case. You can't pick them and you can't change it when it happens. For whatever reasons, the robbery of the Trans was taking over my life.

The summer weeks slipped by, and I made little progress on the case. The other victim of the robbery, 10-year-old Julie moved out of Maine with her mother, and they never returned.

By that point, Don and I could talk about anything. One day I asked him why he did most of the talking and Monica avoided me. Don told me that in their cultures it was customary for the man to do the talking. He also said that Monica was afraid that she would cry if she talked about what happened to Alex.

There it was. That was why Monica seemed so tough, almost cold. She didn't want to show any weakness. Mental toughness had been a requirement for Don and Monica when they were children, and they carried that attribute into adulthood. They had learned to absorb suffering and to move on. That was also something that they passed on to their own children.

Sometimes Alex would ask me if I caught the people that robbed her, and I always told her the same answer.

"Not yet, kiddo, but I will."

Chapter Four

The Academy

I was hoping to get a job as a police officer in Portland or South Portland, and in the summer of 1987 the city to the south of the bridge was giving its entrance exam first. Lucky them.

At the time, I had returned home from overseas, the Army and I had parted ways. I was breezing my way through the college criminal justice courses, taking it all in like a sponge, and I was working for Portland as a police operator. My job was to field incoming calls, write down the type of complaint and hand notes to the dispatchers. It was a fun job but answering phones was not to be my future.

The only thing separating South Portland from Portland was a bridge or two, so I figured the police forces were pretty much the same. At the age of 21 or 22, a young person with a passion for law enforcement just wants a job, and they generally don't care where it happens to be.

Portland is Maine's largest city, with a population of about 80,000. The police department is staffed by 160 officers. I have often said that there are many cities that I have never heard of with more officers than Portland.

South Portland is a small city of about 25,000. It's mainly a bedroom community, but it has its own character. South Portland definitely has a tough streak, a chip on its shoulder.

Back in World War II, thousands of workers came to the South Portland waterfront to build Liberty ships. The shipbuilding companies are gone, but the city still has an industrial feel, with an active railroad yard and a sprawling field of oil tanks that serve the pipeline between Portland Harbor and Montreal. The city also feels bigger than it really is because it's home to the state's largest shopping center, The Maine Mall.

I showed up to take the written exam for South Portland and who is sitting across from me but my old friend Jim Fahey.

We had no idea that the other had applied to the police force. Jim had been letting his hair grow long, drinking way too much and working as a disc jockey in Florida while I was serving in Germany. Of more than 100 people who took the exam that evening, Jim ranked third and I somehow ranked second. I congratulated Jim and looked forward to teaming up with him again; just like our high school days. I was hired in June and he followed suit a few months later. We had come a long way from those endless days of playing pass with a baseball in his back yard. I still think of the pissed-off look on his father's face when we would break yet another slat in the wooden fence, but looking back now we could have been doing a lot worse.

To become a certified police officer in Maine, new hires had to attend the 12-week course at the Criminal Justice Academy. It was located in Waterville then, on a sprawling campus of several large buildings. One housed the recruits and the cafeteria, another had classrooms and another housed the administrative staff and a game room. We stayed at the academy during the week and went home on weekends.

The militaristic approach by the cadre might have worked for some, but not for me.

I had been in the Army, had just gotten out of drill sergeant school and I knew how to march with the best of them. The Maine State Troopers tasked with getting us in shape, uh, didn't. And the treatment that we received was no match for what I had endured under Sergeant Grant at Fort Dix, so I had a hard time taking the approach seriously. Their plan was to tear us down during the first few weeks by hollering and belittling us whenever they could. I was told I had a bad habit of finding humor when they apparently weren't suggesting it.

In chow line, we were forced to stand at attention until we received our food, and of course we weren't allowed to talk.

This was problematic. Inevitably, I would do something to get in trouble and I'd be ushered to the end of the line. Then I'd have to rush my food down – something that I still regret, after years of digestive problems. I got so used to the routine that eventually I just waited for everyone else to line up, then I'd take my rightful place at the end.

Scott Pelletier was usually my partner in crime at chow time. Scott had been hired by the Portland Police Department, and he too had been in the Army, so he wasn't against screwing off as much as he could. His father was an officer, so policing was in his blood, whether he wanted it there or not. We hit it off right away, and I wouldn't wager a bet as to who did more push-ups as punishment during our luxurious stay at MCJA.

I didn't intentionally draw attention to myself, but on occasion it was unavoidable. Every morning we would go outside for physical training. This consisted of a variety of exercises, always wrapped up with a two mile run around the area. I was in pretty good shape so the PT didn't bother me. One recruit was a bit overweight and he consistently dropped out of the run soon after we took off. I started dropping out with him. The guy needed encouragement, someone to run beside.

The trooper didn't see it that way. He shit all over me for being lazy and I put up with the taunting for quite a while. One morning, after the overweight recruit had cut several minutes off his time, I decided to shut this trooper up.

Halfway through the run, I made sure the trooper could see that I had not dropped out, that I was still in formation. Then I took off like a rabbit. This might be a slight exaggeration, but I had showered and had breakfast before the trooper came jogging in. I made my point and nothing needed to be said.

The trooper must have realized that I wasn't screwing off; I was trying to help someone. He also knew I could kick his ass in a run, at least on this day.

Occasionally at the academy, boredom would set in, so a little prank now and then was necessary to keep things lively. One of those pranks involved detection powder, which is purple and very hard to see. Should you sprinkle a small amount on, say, a doorknob or light switch, and then someone touches it, bad things happen. Their skin – and any other skin they have touched – will turn purple when they wash their hands. Not to mention the fact that this stuff doesn't wash off easily with soap.

Tom Roach, an officer who had been hired by Westbrook Police, was getting a bit cocky so I decided to lighten things up by putting just a dash of detection powder on the lamp in his room. It was just a matter of time, and I waited patiently.

Ten minutes later, Tom was bullshit. He was causing quite a scene, accusing everyone he could find. He never suspected me and I never let on that I was the culprit. Tom recently retired from the Westbrook Police Department, and hopefully he doesn't hold grudges.

With only a couple weeks left in the training, I could finally see the light at the end of the tunnel. I had persevered through the endless push-ups, getting caught short-sheeting the cadre's bed, and a few other transgressions. I was ready to get out of there.

But there was one more run-in left. Some genius had decided long ago that certain items were forbidden on academy grounds. These included some necessities like candy, alcohol and pornography. I didn't understand the rule, but I certainly knew it existed.

He appeared in my doorway without notice, standing with his arms crossed – that same trooper that I was forced to outrun a few weeks earlier. Scott Pelletier and I were hanging out during the quiet time after supper and before the shutting down of the lights. The trooper had a strange look on his face that I had not seen before, a blend of anger and disappointment.

Could it have been the pornographic magazine I was reading? Or the Twinkie Scott was eating? Whatever caused the trooper's discontent, I was prepared for the worst. I would take my punishment like a man, as I'm sure Scott would have, but it never came. As Scott went back to chewing and listening to his walkman, and I continued reading, the trooper shook his head and walked away without a word.

We had won. We had defeated his spirit. That's what we thought at the time. I certainly respected the tradition that accompanied the academy, and I thoroughly enjoyed the courses that taught us the laws, techniques, and tactics that would keep us safe. I even liked the cadre who pushed us to our limits. I just had enough and was ready to move on.

In reality, the trooper probably just gave up on us. He saw two young, cocky bastards who were just itching to take on the world, and I'm sure he figured we weren't worth his time or effort. He wanted us out of there and back at our respective departments. We would soon be their problems.

In November of 1987 a photographer memorialized the moment of our academy graduation. The classes actually had been a lot of fun, but I knew that nothing I learned in Waterville could truly prepare me for what I was about to face on the job. I was now a full-fledged police officer eager to hit the streets and turn those blue lights on.

Chapter Five

Rookie years, cocky and clueless

My boots had a shine like they'd never see again when I reported for my first shift as a rookie officer in November of 1987.

I sat down in the classroom where the supervisor passes on pertinent information from the previous shifts. Didn't hear a word he said, but damn I looked good. My shift was 11 p.m. to 7 a.m. and I'd soon learn that only drunks and fighters were awake during those hours, or at least those were the only people I'd have contact with.

Jeff McCue was my sergeant that night. He told me I'd be riding with him, which was fine because I didn't have a clue what I was doing. If I had been asked to respond to a call by myself, I would have been screwed, as I didn't even know the street names.

Jeff drove us down Main Street and we picked up coffees. Not five minutes later we were driving through an industrial section of the city when Jeff saw two enterprising gentlemen stealing a stop sign. I never saw the theft in progress because I was concentrating so hard on not spilling my coffee. First impressions mean a lot.

After giving these two geniuses a summons, Jeff drove straight back to the station, where he typed a brief report and handed it to me. This was his way of showing me how to complete all the necessary paperwork. That was all there was to it. Properly trained, I was now ready to hit the big-time on my own. Jeff handed me the keys. Have a good time.

Those were the good old days, I guess. Officers today have to spend longer – 16 weeks – at that luxury hotel called the police academy. And once they get back to their respective police departments, the rookies face a lengthy training period with their Field Training Officer, or FTO. The new hires are constantly evaluated on policies and procedures, until their supervisors clear them to begin patrol without supervision.

I didn't have the advantage of oversight, but I guess I turned out all right by learning things the hard way. That's a nice way of saying I made a lot of mistakes.

In 1987, the South Portland Police Department had about 50 sworn officers – roughly the same number that the department has today. The shift assignments are based on seniority, and because I had none that meant I'd be on the graveyard shift until some officers retired and others were hired and out of the academy.

If my policing style is a bit unorthodox, and most who know me would call it that, the roots of that style came out of those first few years.

I came to know the local drunks and the street people, the brawlers and the bar-flies. Every city has them; the handful of people that account for the bulk of the calls to police. But I didn't approach them with a tough-guy attitude or a heavy hand. I quickly learned that the best way to diffuse a situation, and to get the type of information that would serve me well later, was to treat everyone with respect. In return, I expected respect from them.

And who was I kidding, anyways? I knew that if my life had veered off in a different direction, if I hadn't caught a couple breaks, I'd be the drunk picking a fight outside the Griffin Club or the American Legion hall.

As someone who has consumed an alcoholic beverage or two on occasion, I felt I had a way of relating to these special people.

There are, of course, limits to compassion.

One time I was dispatched to an old Irish bar for a reported fight outside. It was the middle of the night on St. Patrick's Day, so what could go wrong?

Two ladies, and I use that term loosely, were slapping each other around when I pulled up. One of them was clearly the aggressor. I put her in handcuffs when she refused to stop fighting. She was an attractive woman with dark brown hair. I walked her to my cruiser, and as backup arrived I admired the large crowd gathered outside the bar. I scanned the crowd instead of this angel as I asked her to sit in the back seat. Apparently she didn't want to sit, because she coiled back her tongue and let a large wad of spit fly directly into my face.

That was a particular form of affection that I had never experienced before. It was less than pleasant. I resisted an urge to rap her head off the side of the cruiser, and instead put her in the back seat and hopped in the driver's seat to take her to the jail.

She was calling me names that would have made her mother proud, so I turned around to tell her to shut up. That was another mistake. The Plexiglas divider designed to protect the officer was slid over to the other side of the cruiser, so my new friend took full advantage of that by spitting on the side of my head through the metal cage-wire that separates front seat from back. That really pissed me off.

Another officer was kind enough to sit on this lady as we drove to the jail with her lips facing the floor.

It didn't take long for me to develop a reputation as being a bit of a maverick within the department. I didn't strive for that tag, and I didn't relish it. I just did what I thought was right, and those decisions weren't always popular with my supervisors.

Some rules just didn't make sense. The police chief at the time had a thing about officers wearing their hats when they got out of their cruisers. Chief and the supervisors were really strict on that one. I usually left mine on my seat. It wasn't meant to piss them off, I just felt that the hat was a hindrance to doing my job. Not to mention the fact that it messed up my hair, back when I had some.

I like to think that I practiced community policing before it was in style. That meant I took the time to talk to people who were buying coffee at 3 a.m. I found out what the problems were in the city by listening to what they had to say. Every officer has his or her own way of doing things, and they are all acceptable as long as you stay within the law and department policies. Even in those early days, I wasn't afraid to follow my instincts. The more experience I got, the more unorthodox I became.

I took chances that I had no business taking. I was often the first officer to respond to a complaint about a late night party, and I'd walk into those parties by myself, figuring I could handle it. The thought never crossed my mind that I could get my ass kicked, or worse, if the crowd turned on me. I was turning into a professional bullshitter – figuring out how to get people to do what I wanted them to do, without them ever realizing what was happening.

Decisions were easy for me to make, and they still are. That can be a good attribute for a police officer, but it leaves you open to a lot of second-guessing, and my supervisors did not spare me in that category. Unfortunately, I have never been a politically correct individual, and I didn't keep my mouth shut when I should have. I was in my 20's, stubborn, immature and outspoken. There was a very high standard that I held up for myself, and I had the unrealistic notion that all of my co-workers should be measured by that same bar.

It wasn't until I was suspended for arguing with a supervisor, and sent to a psychiatrist, that I realized I was making things way harder than they needed to be.

We used to watch training videos produced by the Law Enforcement Television Network. One day my supervisor told me I needed to stay in the office and watch a video on trains. He told me not to be afraid to use the fast forward button. So I watched a bit, fast forwarded some, then watched some more. The next day, as I was sitting in one of the police classrooms with a bunch of other officers, the supervisor lit into me. He said I didn't watch the tape, and I was going to stay inside to watch it.

I told him that I watched the tape, and I wasn't going to do it again. That apparently didn't sit well with him, because his voice rose as he told me that it was not a question, it was an order, and that I should sit down and shut up. I believe my quote at that point was, "I'm not your fucking dog, and I'm not going to sit down and shut up."

The supervisor left the room for a few minutes, and when he came back he told me to get my stuff and go home. I picked up my briefcase, put it in my locker, and then went to my parents' house and split a six-pack with my dad. The next day, I went in to speak briefly with the chief. I said I would take a vacation day, to let things cool off, and he agreed.

The next thing I knew, the deputy chief was at my door with two letters. The first told me I was suspended for two days; the second told me I had to see a psychiatrist. In my mind, I had not done anything wrong. The supervisor had called me out in front of everybody, and all I had done was fast-forward a videotape about train crossings. But I went to the doctor as ordered. The first question he asked me was why I had thrown my briefcase across the room during the confrontation with the supervisor.

I told him, you must have the wrong guy. I didn't throw my briefcase. I closed it up and put it in my locker. The psychiatrist looked bewildered, then he disappeared for a few minutes to make a phone call.

Fortunately for me, I had seen the doctor's license plate before our meeting began. It made a reference to fly-fishing. So after he came back and we started our conversation, it quickly turned to one of my favorite activities. You guessed it, my favorite activity was fly fishing even though I had never done it. By the end of the meeting, he was on the couch and I was sitting in his chair. The three page report said that I was sane, but I do have a problem with situations in which I feel wronged, and I have no skills in diplomacy. I could have told the department that and saved them some money.

In the end, I did admit that I was wrong. But I still feel that the supervisor was wrong too. He should have taken me into the office and asked me about the tape, rather than accusing me in front of the whole group.

It was all part of a larger lesson that would take me many more years to fully learn – that I was trying to buck a system that had been in place long before I arrived, and would be there long after I was just a name on an old roster.

Looking back, I can see that my supervisors usually were not only covering their own asses, they were trying to save mine.

Chapter Six

A little help from my friends

Don and Monica Tran were always polite to me, but I'm sure they got sick of hearing my standard line, "I'm still working on it."

I had bits and pieces of the puzzle in my notebooks, but no big breaks and no resources to follow up on the leads that could bring the prosecution of the thugs that had terrorized little Alex and Julie.

Fortunately for me and for them, in the fall of 1998 – about four months after the robbery – I was about to get the clout of the federal government behind me.

I had only been a detective for a short time, but my lieutenant, Gerard "Butch" Guimond, had recommended me for a special assignment. He volunteered me to serve on a Violent Crime Task Force that had just been established by the U.S. Justice Department.

The task force would be comprised of officers from the various local and regional police departments, and the mission was to investigate violent felonies in the Portland area.

One day that fall, Lt. Guimond and I attended a meeting at the U.S. Attorney's Office in Portland. The conference room table was surrounded by brass and chiefs from local police departments. You can imagine how I felt as I squirmed in my seat. These chiefs were all sitting straight up so their expensive suits didn't get wrinkled, and there were only three of us who looked like we walked over from the homeless shelter.

There was Mike Saenz, who introduced himself as an agent from the Bureau of Alcohol, Tobacco and Firearms. And there was Rob Nichols, a Maine State Trooper. Hell, I could have told everybody that before the introductions, just by looking at his haircut.

Jon Chapman, an assistant U.S. attorney, led the meeting. He was a fairly short man with a full head of hair, which made me jealous right away. My hair started slipping out shortly after I got out of the Army, but luckily I was tall, and I couldn't see my own bald spot.

Chapman took the reins and told everybody how great the federal government was, and how this task force was about to deal a major blow to violent crime in greater Portland. He was well spoken and impressive, and I felt that if his legal career were to fail, he could easily score a job as a bullshit artist.

I listened as the chiefs told Chapman how great the task force idea was, but they generally followed that up with "But we just don't have the manpower to commit anybody to it."

It was finally time for Butch Guimond to speak and I held my breath. Guimond was not shy in the least. He said what he had to say, how he wanted to say it, and he didn't give a damn who he was saying it to. I liked that guy a lot.

I slouched down low as Guimond stood on his soapbox. Not only was the task force a great idea, he said, but South Portland was committing an officer to the force, and he pointed down at me.

He encouraged all of these officers who outranked him to find a way to commit officers, too. This went over like a fart in church, and when the meeting ended I realized that this big federal task force, which was about to kick some serious ass, consisted of Mike Saenz, Rob Nichols and yours truly. We were off to a fabulous start.

Our office was in a little hole directly above the U.S. Attorney's Office. The way I looked at it, we didn't need much room because we didn't have any cases.

Of course, I had just the case to get us going. I brought the entire case file on the Tran robbery into the office and presented it to the guys.

Mike and I saw eye to eye from the beginning. I knew that this was someone who would become a lifelong ally and friend. He was easygoing and down to earth and he lacked that 'holier-than-thou' attitude that a lot of federal agents have. Mike's family was from El Salvador, and he spent several years working for the police department in Dallas, Texas, before he was hired by ATF in the late 1980's.

I've worked with countless federal agents over the years and most of them are outstanding people and investigators. Some didn't live up to expectations, and I have my own theory on that. A guy who gets a four-year degree and then gets hired by an agency is at a serious disadvantage. They haven't had the life experiences, the opportunities to learn what makes people tick. They get their training at some federal facility and off to work they go solving crimes.

It's tough to understand a drunk if you've never had a drink, tough to handle a domestic situation if you've never argued with your partner, tough to get someone to tell you what they don't want to tell you, if you have never practiced the art of interviewing. These are the things that street level pavement-pushing officers do on a daily basis.

As for Rob Nichols, he was one of the nicest guys I've ever met, but I think he would be the first to admit that conducting investigations was not his specialty. He could never hide the fact that he was a state trooper, through and through. He walked like a trooper, talked like a trooper, and he still is a trooper. I'll never forget how excited he was to be assigned an undercover vehicle, a Cadillac. He was the cat's meow in that thing. He often wore brightly colored Hawaiian shirts to work, but they never made sense with his high-and-tight haircut.

Rob had to commute on the Maine turnpike everyday, and he had quite a drive. One day Rob strolled into the office proudly reporting that he had stopped a guy for speeding on the way in. I was imagining what that poor speeder thought when he saw Rob walking up, looking like a white Don Ho. Most police officers that work undercover pretty much forget they are officers. What I mean is that we don't notice those speeders, we drive right by accidents unless someone is injured, and we could give a damn if a drunk is in someone's face unless it's ours. Rob never forgot what he was, and for that I would always commend him.

Jon Chapman, Mike, Rob and I sat around a table and reviewed the Tran case. I was looking for suggestions on where to go next. We all decided that I should go have another heart to heart with my favorite teenagers – Jessica and Alicia.

Jessica and Alicia had returned to Maine and those angels were once again living under the roof of their mother, Mary, in Scarborough.

By that point I had developed a bit of a rapport with Mary. She was a single mom who liked to flirt, and I had no problem playing along. I called her and told her I needed to speak with the girls again, and Mary told me she'd have the coffee on when I got there.

I asked Mike to come along and bring the weight of the federal government with him. As always, he was accommodating, but he didn't know what he was in for. We walked in and Mary, Jessica and Alicia filled that kitchen with loud, entertaining conversation. I let the girls think they were something special until I couldn't take their line of bullshit anymore. I explained to them exactly how serious this investigation was, and that if they held anything back, or lied to us, they could get in trouble, too.

Slowly, I think the girls started to get it. My notebook was filling up with what sounded like good information – some small pieces to a puzzle.

Jessica and Alicia took the bus to North Carolina to visit "T", the younger brother of Paula, who was Monica's sister-in-law. They had met "T", Paula and Kieu when all of them were in Maine, and the girls were getting their nails done at Monica and Don's shop. Jessica and Alicia arrived in North Carolina the same day as the robbery occurred. Kieu and another young man named Tola picked them up.

Kieu and Paula told the girls that "T" was visiting friends in Charlotte, but that he would be back soon. That struck Jessica and Alicia as odd, since the whole point of their trip was to visit him.

Turns out the girls did have vivid memories of their trip to North Carolina, and I wasn't pleased that it took them so long to share those memories with me. They remembered a group of men arriving at Kieu's home a few days after they got there. One of the men was chubby and had tattoos on his hand. Another had a mole on the side of his face. I recalled my interviews with Alex and Julie; those men were a match for the robbers that had terrorized the little girls.

Jessica and Alicia also remembered a car that some of the men drove – a tan Honda Accord. Taking a minute to flip through my notes from the day of the robbery, I knew that this was leading to the right place. Way down in the corner of a page I saw the words "Tan Honda Accord." One of the residents at the Trans' apartment complex had seen some Asian men hanging around and they thought that was the make of car they were driving.

My favorite teenagers also said the guy with the mole on his face drove a different car that had broken down. They didn't know the make or model, but they knew it was white. The girls eventually saw the light and realized the seariousness of my investigation. Their cooperation improved greatly as the case progressed. We actually ended up getting along great as they grew older and matured.

This group of men only stayed at Kieu's for a few days, and then they piled into the Honda headed for Atlanta, which is where they said they were from. It sounded like the home of Kieu and Paula was a revolving door for a lot of people during the week that Jessica and Alicia stayed there.

The girls said one of the Asian men had bought the Honda Accord from a friend of Kieu's named Tony. I focused in on that car and made several phone calls to authorities down in North Carolina, seeking the identity of the man who sold it and the one who bought it. Finally I tracked down Tony and spoke with him on the phone. He didn't provide much for information, but he confirmed that the man who bought the Honda lived in Atlanta. His name was Sang Tran.

Each day I had been conferring with Mike Saenz and Jon Chapman. They had to be sick of my incessant talking about this case. Over coffee with Mike one morning I laid all my cards on the table. I was spinning my wheels and racking up one hell of a phone bill.

Of course I knew what had to be done, but I didn't think it was possible. I had to go to Atlanta and track these guys down.

It always comes down to money. I had already approached the South Portland chief and he told me flat-out that the department couldn't afford to pay for the trip. So I glanced over at Mike during our chat. Would ATF send me to Atlanta? I was expecting him to laugh in my face, but he didn't. That was the day I learned how much deeper the pockets of the federal government are. Mike not only got approval for me to travel to Atlanta, but he was approved to travel with me and to help with this investigation that was beginning to drive me crazy.

The Trans were ecstatic, and I was determined not to come back from Atlanta without answers, despite all the obvious barriers. It was a huge city, an unfamiliar place, and in the neighborhoods where we would be going, the people practiced different customs and spoke different languages.

To say that we would be searching for needles in a haystack would be an understatement.

But as Mike and I flew out of Portland on Feb. 28, 1999, I couldn't dwell on the odds. All I had to do was shut my eyes and remember the sound of Alex's voice as she asked me if I would catch the robbers, and my own voice telling her that I would.

Chapter Seven

Losing my father,
and a piece of myself

You get a bit cold, a bit hard to the world when you choose to become a police officer. You have to. Otherwise your heart would simply break.

There are suicides, sexual assaults, armed robberies and gruesome car crashes.

The thing that always gets you, though, is the kids. Kids growing up in the chaos, moving from filthy apartment to filthy apartment. Kids with welfare moms and prison dads, parents who are too consumed with their own problems or vices, or just too distracted to give a damn. Hungry kids who need more food and more love in their lives, and as an officer you know that it's not going to get any better.

It was hard for me to see that world. I had grown up wanting nothing, with two hardworking, loving parents who put my needs first. I had to learn that those things I had accepted as normal – stability, consistent care and discipline – were not normal for every child. Police and courts can't end the cycle. My heart always aches for those kids, and I do what I can just to make their lives a bit more bearable.

After just two years on the late shift, I had seen more cases of abuse, neglect and domestic violence than I knew existed beneath the familiar slogan that tells people that Maine represents "the way life should be."

My chance to move to the second shift arrived earlier than I thought it would, two years after joining the force. The economy was good then, so officers were retiring in 1989. They were more concerned with getting the hell out of there than they were about hanging on to their health benefits. So I began my eight-year stint on the 3 p.m. to 11 p.m. shift.

For some reason, I expected the sky to open and for sunshine to pour into my life when I finally got to sleep like a normal person. Well, that didn't exactly happen.

I definitely wasn't the favored son of the South Portland Police Department. I wasn't a big fan of my supervisors, and they certainly weren't big fans of mine. I didn't look for trouble, but I certainly didn't back down from it. So I muddled through my shifts one by one and tried to remain out of sight and out of my bosses' minds.

Even though I was enjoying my work, something was definitely missing. I couldn't put my finger on it, but I wasn't as happy as I should have been. That was different for me, someone who has always been an optimist. My mother always told me that it's easier to smile than frown.

Every day after work I'd drive home to the little house I bought from my grandfather. I wouldn't say it was in the best neighborhood, but it was mine. I had a little dog that I named Rags, because I went through a lot of them before he decided to stop shitting on my floor. Rags was a stray that I rescued from the animal shelter when he was a puppy. He looked like a German Shephard, but he was shortchanged in the legs department. He grew to weigh all of 50 pounds, but despite his faults he was a great companion.

Those were my single days when Rags had free roam of the house, and as long as he kept his ass out of my face, he was allowed in the bed. Needless to say, those days, and poor Rags himself, are long gone.

Right around the time when I moved to the second shift was when my father got sick.

Donald Webster was a regular guy, and my hero at the same time. He grew up on Riverside Street in Portland, and in the 1960's he wanted badly to become a police officer. But they had a height requirement in those days, and dad came up just a bit short. Go down the hall to the Fire Department, he was told.

So in 1966, when I was about a year old, he joined the Portland Fire Department. For the next 20 years he worked for the department, and he painted and hung wallpaper on the side.

Sometimes he would work all night at the fire station, come home, change his clothes and go paint all day. Then he would come home to eat dinner, shower and change before heading back to the fire station again. He hardly slept, and he didn't have much leisure time, but I knew that he did it all for my mom, myself and my sister.

My dad rose to the rank of deputy chief, but he never talked much about work or his promotions. He loved being assigned to ladder six, he loved working on the rescue, and his favorite place was when he was assigned to captain the fire boat.

The funny thing is, with all the work he did, dad always found time to take me fishing or to play a game of catch in the front yard. It didn't matter how tired he was.

My father loved life. He had a captivating smile, an infectious laugh and a unique charm about him. In general he was a quiet man, but he and I always got along, and I never felt there was anything more that I needed from him. He was even-tempered and I only remember him raising his voice a few times, and boy did I deserve those.

My parents got along great. Later in his career, he and my mom took vacations to Las Vegas together.

In 1986, he took the job as the first full-time fire chief for the town of Cape Elizabeth. The town needed him to be closer than my parents' house in Westbrook, so they moved to a house in South Portland. That worked out well for me, because once I started working second shift as a South Portland police officer, I would go most nights to my parent's house for supper.

I'll never forget the day I stopped at my parents' house for supper and saw my mother's ashen face at the door.

"Your father has cancer," she said.

"Can they fix it?" I asked.

"They don't know," she said.

I tried to act like a tough guy. I ate what I could of my supper and went back to work. I never saw my dad that night because he was upstairs throwing up. He was only 46 years old.

For the next several years, my dad fought prostate cancer like the champion he was. He still had that same smile, but he wasn't the same. If the doctors had caught it even a month earlier, they might have saved his life. But by the time of the diagnosis, he had cancer spreading all through his body and there was no stopping it.

So he did what anyone in his shoes would do. He bought a new boat. We shared many a six pack of his favorite beverage, Miller beer.

"You want to go fishing?" he would ask me.

"Yep," I'd say.

We hunted together, too. He bought a piece of land in Avon when my sister and I were still little, and I remember him letting me help him build the hunting camp.

Radiation therapy was awful. I would pick him up in the morning, take him to the hospital, and on the way back home we would stop for breakfast. I saw him wilting away and it was tough to accept.

One night in early 1992, we went out and had a beer. He said he didn't feel well, and he wanted to go home. The next day he was in the hospital. I visited him on Feb. 14, my birthday. That was the last day I saw him alive. A few days later he had a brain aneurysm, and by the time I got to the hospital, he was gone. In my mind, that aneurysm was a blessing. He could have laid in that bed for weeks or months, getting sicker and sicker. But he went quickly, just like that, and I will always be grateful. Donald Webster was 50 years old and in the prime of his life when he ascended the stairs to heaven.

For me, the days that followed were tough. Like any other son I grieved the loss of my father. It's purely a selfish reaction. You miss that person and you want one more chance to speak to him or hold them close. Memories can't hug you; memories can't talk to you or love you.

As I grieved, I also made it a point to keep my composure, and that is exactly what I did through the wake and in the days before the funeral.

I remember turning onto Congress Street in Portland that morning, and seeing the two fire trucks with their ladders crossed high above the roadway. The sight took my breath away. I hadn't fully understood until then the majesty with which firemen honor their fallen brothers. The tribute reiterated the fact that my dad was a great guy who had a lot of friends.

Hundreds of people filled the Chestnut Street United Methodist Church, an old congregation still dominated by Italian families. I was the rock that I thought I had to be. No tears, stiff shoulders, a beacon of strength.

I only made one mistake. I turned around and saw one of my father's best friends crying like a baby. That's when I lost it. We're not talking red eyes; I sobbed uncontrollably for several minutes.

It sunk in at what I felt was the most inconvenient moment. My best friend, mentor, and dad was not coming back.

A piece of me died when my father did, so I worked with a heavy heart during those next years on the second shift. I knew he would want me to prosper, so I tried to look forward and to remember the good times, rather than dwell on the bad ones.

I sold the hunting camp in Avon to a bunch of friends, so I could still go if I wanted to. But I don't.

That was for me and him, and I want to remember it just like that.

Chapter Eight

Maggie and Bill

"The fear of death follows from the fear of life. A man who lives fully is prepared to die at any time." – Mark Twain.

I've never been a traffic hound. Those are the cops that pull over every car with a burnt-out tail light or dirty license plate. I was usually too busy shooting the bull with somebody, or answering those mundane calls for service.

But there was one night in the mid-1990's that I actually stopped a car in the No Arrest Time Zone, commonly referred to as the NATZ. This time zone began about one hour before our shift was due to end. Nobody wanted to get stuck with paperwork just before beer time. As a driver in South Portland you had to do something pretty bad to get locked up during the NATZ.

This one car, though, I had to stop because he almost hit me head-on on a one-way street. I walked up to the driver. He was elderly, probably in his mid-80s. He was very pleasant as he explained that he was trying to get to his girlfriend's house near the ocean. I thought, more power to him for having a girlfriend at his age.

The nice man told me his girlfriend's name was Maggie. I gave him a personal escort to her house, so he wouldn't get lost again. Maggie's house was blacker than the ace of spades. I knocked on the door anyway, because my new friend told me that he really needed to talk to Maggie.

This sweet little lady eventually opened the door just enough so I could see one of her eyes. I told her that her boyfriend had gotten lost, and I was the gallant officer who helped him find his way. She looked at me like I had a third eye in the middle of my forehead.

"What boyfriend?" she said. "I don't have a boyfriend."

By that point, Bill was making his way toward the door. I guessed Maggie was in her 70's. She had bushy gray hair and a gentle, calming voice. She kindly told Bill that it was really late, that he should go home and that she would call him the next day. Dejected, Bill agreed, and he got back into his car and drove off.

After Bill left, Maggie invited me inside and we sat talking at her cluttered kitchen table. She explained that a friend had introduced her to Bill only a few days earlier. They had gone out to dinner, but Maggie was concerned by his behavior. He seemed possessive, and obviously wanted more out of the relationship than she did.

"At my age," Maggie told me, "the last thing that I need is a boyfriend."

I decided not to argue that point with her. She then told me that Bill had also grabbed her hard by the wrist and left a bruise, and she did not feel he was thinking straight. Bill had been a teacher earlier in life, and his wife had died a few months earlier.

Maggie told me she was going to visit a friend for a few days, so she would not have to worry about Bill. To me, it sounded like an excellent idea, and I left the house thinking that the problem was solved.

Three days later, at the start of my shift, a dispatcher sent me to Maggie's house. Bill was parked out front, sitting in his car, and Maggie obviously didn't want him there.

I pulled up and asked Bill what he was doing. He stepped out of his car, wearing dress pants and a windbreaker. He really wanted to talk to Maggie, but said he couldn't find her. Apparently he did not realize she was inside.

I decided to have a heart to heart with Bill. Maggie liked him, I said, but she wasn't ready for a steady relationship. He listened, but I don't know if he heard what I was saying. I suggested that he should go home and relax, or take a walk. It was a beautiful day outside. Bill stood there with his hands in the pockets of his windbreaker. He put his head down, said "OK," got into his car and drove away.

Maggie thanked me for not letting Bill into her house. He had left several strange messages on her machine while she was away, and Maggie was nervous. She also handed me a single key and told me that Bill had given it to her. Maggie asked me to return it. With nothing else to do, I figured I would pay Bill a visit to return the key and to make sure he was doing all right.

Bill's house was only a few miles away, and when I pulled into the driveway I was thinking that it looked like a grandfather's house. It was a ranch-style home, with green shutters that needed a coat of paint. A large barn out back was probably used just for storage. The picket fence that enclosed the yard needed repair, too.

His car was there, but no sign of Bill. I walked to the side door and knocked. No answer. It was strange, considering that I couldn't have been more than five minutes behind him. I figured that he took me up on the suggestion to take a walk, so I got back in my cruiser and backed out of the driveway.

Just as I was driving away, something on the front lawn caught my eye. I got out again and walked toward the fence. That's when I saw him. At first I felt terrible because I thought he fell in the yard. Then I got closer.

People who take their own lives with a gun have a tendency to land in awkward positions. It was like that for Bill. Standing over his body I could see the entrance wound on the right side of his head and the exit wound on the left. The bullet was lying on the ground next to his head as if it had done its damage and simply dropped out.

Bill, no doubt a man of honor and dignity who probably spent most of his life teaching and taking care of others, couldn't stand to live his own life anymore.

He must have had that gun, which was still in the tight grip of his right hand, inside his windbreaker when I spoke to him in front of Maggie's house. I don't know whether he made the right choice that afternoon, but I remember thinking that he sure as hell made the right decision by not ending Maggie's life, or mine.

I waited there until the medical examiner arrived and Bill was taken to a funeral home. I told them to take good care of him. Don't ask me how you take good care of a dead man, but it seemed like the right thing to say.

It was even tougher returning to Maggie's house. She cried, I held her hand and we just sat together for a while. I stopped in every now and then to check on Maggie. I think she enjoyed the company and she made a great cup of coffee. I don't know if she is still alive or if she still lives at that house. She was a very nice lady, one of the many I met while working on the second shift.

A lot of older people get lonely and they just want to talk for a while with someone they can trust. I don't think that's too much to ask in your golden years.

On the night of the suicide, I drove to my mother's house for dinner. I'm glad she was close, so I could visit with her and get some of that home cooking that I enjoyed as a kid. I told my mother about my friends Bill and Maggie, and I sat down at the table and ate a great big dish of spaghetti and meatballs.

This is the life of a policeman.

Chapter Nine

Grave topplers and a cross-dressing con man

Feb. 14, 1997
Headline: THREE BOYS CAUGHT TOPPLING STONES
Police say they suspected youths were knocking over the gravestones, but had no idea the offenders would be so young

In my early years as a cop, I never imagined that I would become a detective. For better or worse, that's exactly what happened.

In 1997, ten years into my career, I found myself standing in a hallway at police headquarters, face to face with Lt. Butch Guimond. There had been a shake-up within the force, and a position was open in the detective bureau.

"Are you putting in for it?" Guimond asked.

I thought he had lost his mind. A lot of patrol officers would be putting in for that spot, and I wasn't exactly the Golden Child of the South Portland PD.

But for whatever reason, Guimond was certain that I'd do a good job.

That night I talked it over with my wife. We had our three children by then, and we had moved from the little house that was my grandfather's to a bigger, nicer house in a different suburb of Portland.

Debbie wanted to stay home with the kids, so my hours at work would be flexible. She helped me realize that I had paid my dues on patrol. I had been hit, kicked, spit on and shit on long enough, and a change of scenery might do me good.

I was never a person who could let things go very easily, so I thought that would be an asset as a detective.

Eight patrolmen applied, and when the interviews were done, I was the pick.

I found out later that the chief questioned the decision – I'm guessing that was because of my past indiscretions and the fact that I had been written up more than once – but Lt. Guimond and another supervisor went to bat for me. They told the chief that if I screwed up royally, he could always demote me.

Looking back on it, that move was the new beginning I had been waiting for.

It started off with a bang. A few weeks into the new assignment, my boss tracked me down and handed me a piece of paper with a name and address written on it. He said that several headstones had been knocked over at a local cemetery, and this man wanted to help us stop the damage.

My boss told me to do whatever I needed to do to catch the vandals, and he reminded me how pissed off people get when the graves of their loved ones are desecrated.

The man met me in his driveway. He told me that some kids liked to cut through the back of the cemetery, and then through his property, after school. He didn't have proof, but he suspected they were the ones toppling the headstones.

He looked at his watch. It was just about time for school to let out. He pointed to his backyard, which was covered in at least two feet of snow, and suggested we take a walk. I looked down at my feet.

I had on my finest suit that I recently bought at S&K Menswear; my new loafers still had that fresh smell of leather.

I was thinking there was no way in hell I was getting those new shoes wet. Being a new detective and all, though, I decided to follow his lead. He trudged ahead of me in his L.L. Bean boots. I followed behind in my loafers.

We crested a small hill, the cemetery's high point.

"What the hell is that," I said, stopping the man in mid-stride.

Sure enough, three young boys were walking, kicking

headstones along the way. They looked to be about 11 or 12 years old.

"Hey," I yelled at them.

They froze. With nowhere to run to, they walked slowly toward us.

After an angry lecture that lasted for several minutes, I returned each of those model citizens to their parents. They admitted to all of the damage – nearly 50 headstones that would cost thousands of dollars to replace.

My boss was ecstatic. I was a goddamned hero that day. The local news ran the story of how this diligent policeman caught these kids in the act. It wasn't that big a deal to me, but apparently it was to the relatives of those who had been laid to rest in that cemetery.

Of course, it was the concerned resident who was the real hero. I didn't tell too many people that if the man hadn't forced me off my ass and into the snow, I never would have seen those kids.

A few months later I saw an advertisement from a utility company that was taking nominations for good samaritans. I put this man's name in for one of their awards, and he won. He invited his entire family to the ceremony and there was a smile on his face from the moment I got there to the moment I left. I hoped that my boss wouldn't expect all of my cases to go so smoothly.

Large police departments have specialized units. Robbery. Homicide. Burglary. But if you work for a department like South Portland, you need to be pretty good at many things, but specialize in none.

As I settled into the job, time moved fast. I went from case to case and I loved it. I had the opportunity to deal with victims who needed my help, and suspects who proved to be worthy adversaries. Slowly I learned the art of interviewing, and I was also learning how to think outside the box in order to solve a crime.

I had a passion for my work that I had not experienced in a

long time. It wasn't that I got a kick out of arresting people and taking them to jail; for me, it was the hunt. I approached the more meaningful cases as a problem, and I was driven to solve those problems no matter where they took me.

One of the more peculiar cases I worked on involved a scam artist who came to Maine "from away," as we like to say here.

In the fall of 1997, we started to get complaints about teenagers soliciting money for a supposed charitable organization. The Maine Substance Abuse Council, residents were told, was a non-profit agency that raised money to help people suffering from drug addiction. The organization had a 24-hour hotline, but no one ever answered the phone.

It didn't take me long to figure out something was rotten about this agency. I talked to a couple of the kids who were raising the money, who told me the name of one man who ran the operation. Armed with a search warrant, I showed up at the office of the Maine Substance Abuse Council, which was on a second floor above a construction company, and consisted of a couple tables and a telephone.

After walking up the stairs I was greeted by a couple of tough-looking teenagers who obviously had not expected the police. I noticed a couple of doors that had padlocks on them. One of the kids said the director had gone to the store.

I didn't have to wait long to be entertained. As I watched this gentleman walk in I immediately thought of Tiny Tim singing "Tip-toe through the Tulips." Mr. Walsh was around 50 years old, with curly hair and a pear-shaped body. His hands looked as though he had recently received a manicure.

When I asked this entrepreneur if he had the keys to the padlocks, he said no. Then I motioned to another officer to kick the doors in, and suddenly he remembered the keys were in his pocket.

I was hoping for a bundle of cash or some other evidence of serious wrongdoing. What I got was a closet full of size 13 women's shoes, dresses that would fit a linebacker, and accessories that every cross dresser needs to complete his wardrobe. It was nice stuff, but not for me. There was definitely some giggling in the room. I have nothing against those who choose alternative lifestyles, but I also reserve the right to find such things entertaining.

Having seen a light pink strapless dress with matching high-heeled shoes, it was tough to talk to the blue-jeans wearing Mr. Walsh.

That became even more difficult when we found pictures of our new friend modeling some of the most intimate apparel. For a guy like me with a twisted sense of humor, this was a good night. Of course we also found what we were looking for – proof that the council was nothing more than Mr. Walsh's cash machine. Turns out this guy was a convicted felon and a recovering drug addict, and he was headed back to jail. I'm sure that the parents of those kids working for him wouldn't want them associating with such a stellar businessman.

Chapter Ten

Chasing the clues in Atlanta

Approaching Hartsfield Airport in Atlanta, I was amazed by the red clay that dominated the landscape. It was late February of 1999 and the warm weather was a welcome break from the sub-zero temperatures that we were accustomed to in Maine.

I had only been to Atlanta once before, when one of my Army buddies got married. It was a completely different world from South Portland. Mike Saenz and I were going in with hopes a lot higher than actual expectations, but we both knew that the answers to our questions about the Tran robbery could only be answered here.

We discussed our plan of action during the flight, and decided to start out by endearing ourselves to the local police officers, and begging them for help.

I thought we would be able to walk into Atlanta Police headquarters, talk to a detective and get all the help we needed. That didn't quite work out. I soon realized that there were a lot of police departments in and around the city that I had never heard of, and we would be depending on their good will.

I also spent hours formulating a game plan. Out of all the witnesses and possible suspects in the robbery, who would be the weakest link? Who could we realistically hope to find quickly?

In my mind the answer was Rithy Kiev, the teenager also known as "T." Rithy was the kid brother of Paula, Monica Tran's sister-in-law. He had mysteriously been out of town when Alicia and Jessica traveled from Maine to North Carolina to visit him at Paula and Kieu's house. And he lived in the Atlanta area with his parents.

I needed to interview Rithy, but I was concerned because he was still a juvenile. I didn't come all the way to Georgia to have some parent tell me that I couldn't talk to his kid.

One of our first stops was the Clayton County Police Department. We sat down with an older black detective who just shook his head when he learned we had come all the way from Maine to investigate a home invasion robbery. At first this put me off, until he explained how many robberies of this type happen within his jurisdiction alone. He also told us that dozens of these robberies happen each year without ever being reported.

I realized how lucky I was that Don and Monica Tran called the police in the first place, and cared enough to stick with the process for month after agonizing month. I also realized how lucky the girls were to walk away with only mental scars.

This old time detective in Clayton County gave us some advice before we went on our merry way, chasing our tails. It was the same advice that I had received from another urban detective the day after the robbery.

He told us that Asian suspects often refused to talk to police. If I was able to get an interview, the suspect would only talk if we showed him that we had overwhelming evidence, and that he was screwed. If I tried to bluff the suspect into a confession – without having the information I needed – I might as well not even try.

First we needed to find Rithy, and I wanted to interview him as a witness, not as a suspect. This much I did know about Rithy: He wasn't one of the actual robbers, because he didn't match the descriptions that Alex gave me. Also, he was still a kid in the eyes of the court system, so even if he had done something wrong he would probably end up with a big slap on the wrist.

Just before dark on March 1, Mike and I found the house belonging to Rithy's parents, in a neat subdivision in College Park. I was impressed by the neighborhood, having imagined that we'd be going to some run-down project where the tires would be stolen from our rental car.

A short kid answered the door, and I knew it was Rithy because I had been looking at pictures of him for the past several months. He got that nervous look in his eyes real quick when we introduced ourselves. But he let us in, and told us he was home alone. How perfect. I tried to get a feel for the kid as we walked downstairs and sat down. He didn't make much eye contact and spoke softly, so I knew immediately that he had something to tell us. It was sinking in for Rithy that two cops from Maine were in his house. I had to tread lightly because I had no idea if his sister Paula was involved in the crime, and I figured he wouldn't implicate her.

I decided to go with the know-it-all approach, where I suggest that the case is basically wrapped up and I just need to get his side of the story. I laid a few of my cards on the table and the kid took the bait.

I used everything in my power to remain stoic when I heard what came out of Rithy's mouth over the next few minutes.

Rithy said he didn't know the other guys were going to rob anyone. He only drove with them to Maine because they said he had to.

Turns out the older men needed Rithy because he had been to the Tran's apartment in South Portland, and he could show them where it was.

I glanced over at Mike. Like me, I could tell he was suppressing a big grin. We knew that our trip to Georgia had just paid off. Rithy told us that he was with his sister Paula and her boyfriend Kieu in Buford, Georgia, when they met up with four Asian men. He didn't know their full names, but he was able to provide some information about them and the trip to Maine. It was pretty clear that this wasn't a violent kid.

Leaving Rithy behind, our next step was to find Sang Tran, the man who was supposedly connected to the tan Honda Accord described by witnesses.

As luck would have it, Sang Tran was home at his apartment in Atlanta on the afternoon of March 3. The bad news was that his English was just as good as my Vietnamese. He was a small man who seemed to have a smile that wouldn't go away. Mike and I kept trying to explain why we were there, and Sang just kept smiling at us, shaking his head. This guy had no idea what we were talking about, and I had a pretty good feeling he'd never even run a stop sign, let alone tie some kids up. After several minutes and some success in getting beyond the language barrier, Sang told us that his former roommate, Dung Tran, had tried to sell him a tan Honda Accord sometime in the summer of 1998.

The Asian community in Atlanta is huge, but I figured it couldn't hurt to ask Sang a long shot question: Did Dung Tran have any friends that drove a white car?

He came up with a name of a man who lived near Asian Square in Atlanta, and was friends with Dung Tran. The guy drove a white car, and Sang heard a rumor that he was doing time in jail.

The man's name, Sang told us, was Thong Nguyen.

Chapter Eleven

Lies, truth and the art of an interview

Aug. 21, 1998
**Headline: BANK ROBBER GETS 4 1/2 YEARS IN PRISON
IN LIGHT OF THREATS Richard Gray did not cooperate
with police after the ill-planned heist of two local banks last
April.**

Most people are not convincing liars.

And when they lie, there's almost always a physical "tell" that gives them away.

Sometimes it's the most obvious one, eye contact. This goes back to when we were little kids. When you did something wrong and your father was interrogating you, where did your eyes go when you tried to blame it on your brother or sister? More than likely you stared at your shoes, or at the photo of Aunt Gertrude hanging on the wall, while you wished you were someplace else. Some habits die hard.

Other signs are more subtle. Some people sweat, or rub their hands together, or tap their feet. It's part of my job to figure out the tell, and use it to my advantage. I learned to ask questions that were designed to elicit a response that I was pretty sure would be a lie, just so I could see if any mannerisms stuck out.

In my first few years as a detective I interviewed hundreds of suspects, witnesses and victims. I listened, watched and learned. If someone does something long enough, they should start to get pretty good at it, and that's how I felt about myself as a detective. I began to excel at reading people, communicating with them and getting the information that I needed to do my job. I knew I had a lot more to learn, but I was getting there.

It's never enough to simply know if a suspect is lying. You have to be able to understand where the person is coming from. You have to know what motivated them to commit the crime in the first place. If you can identify that motivation, and relate to the suspect about it, that's when you get the confession.

I think that most people on this earth have a soul and at least a slice of a conscience. If someone does something he shouldn't do, he still wants a chance to explain why he did it. The premise is no different if you steal a candy bar, sell a kilo of cocaine or kill your own sister. The stakes might be higher, but the psychological premise is the same.

While every suspect is unique and I approach every interview with that in mind, there is one common theme I bring to all of them: Be nice. I want that person on the other side of the table to like me. If there's one cop who treats you like the dope that you are, and the other cop seems to care deeply about your situation, who would you confess your sins to?

I have no problem putting on a show during an interview. I can bring myself to tears if necessary, or I can put my feet up on my desk and downplay the situation. I have shaken the nastiest hands and nudged the smelliest people to get them to a place in their minds where they feel comfortable enough to talk to me.

I should mention a few things I never do in an interview. I don't make shit up. If the suspect is a champion bowler and I can't hit a single pin, I'm not going to pretend we played in the same league.

Also, I never promise a suspect something if I don't intend on following through. If you tell some asshole that you'll take his sister to the prom if he turns himself in, then you'd better be getting measured for a tuxedo after he turns up at the jail.

One mistake that some police officers make when interviewing someone is to jump right into the barrel. They start off by asking the person all about the crime they are suspected of committing. This rarely works. You have to build trust, which most often comes out of shared experience. Over the years I have told people that I have no kids, or that I have five kids. I've said my parents were both dead, and someone probably still thinks that my parents manage a nude beach and spa in West Texas. You could use your imagination and wonder about some of the stories I've come up with.

All of this might sound manipulative, and to a certain degree it is. But the intent is to find out the truth. And ultimately, that is the best thing not only for the victims of crime, but for the suspects I interview. The Supreme Court ruled years ago that it "is" ok for the police to lie and use deception in certain circumstances.

The faster they admit what they've done, suffer the legal consequences and move on toward healing, the better shot they have at redemption in life.

Some of the interviews that I am most prepared for are the ones that don't take any longer than a few minutes.

One of those happened in the spring of 1998. I was at home one day when my supervisor called and asked me to come in early. Two bank robberies within minutes of each other was enough to get me off the couch.

Some guy had gone into a bank in the Millcreek area of the city, which is a nice mix of retail stores, restaurants, parks and homes. He walked up to a teller and demanded money. Unimpressed, the teller simply walked away, and the would-be robber left the bank. Refusing to be deterred by failure, this genius gathered his remaining wits and walked across the street to another bank. That time he walked out with $12,000 in cash. I guess persistence pays off.

I interviewed the tellers and did what I do, but made little progress that first day. It was also the first time that I had the unique experience of working alongside the Federal Bureau of Investigation. Most banks are federally insured, so that brings bank robberies into the FBI's bailiwick. Don't get me wrong, that doesn't mean the agency does all the work, it just gets them involved.

When the FBI agent, the primary investigator on the robberies, decided to go home at 4 p.m. that day, I was more than a little frustrated. There was a lot more that could have been done, and should have been done, right away. It's one of those obvious tenets of law enforcement – a crime gets harder and harder to solve as time passes. I wasn't mad at the FBI agent, who was a great guy, just frustrated because my personality urged me to push on. He answered to a different boss and I understood that.

The next day we beat the bushes, talking to anyone who might have information. We showed people photos from the bank surveillance cameras. One of the local kids happened to be walking through the area, so the guy I was riding with and I showed him the photos.

He studied it for a minute and told us that it looked like Rick Ray. He said Rick was a guy he had met a few times around town. The jail didn't have anyone in their records matching Rick Ray, but they did have a record for a Richard Gray. The age was about right, so I decided to take a ride over to the jail to look at his old booking photo. One look at that photo and I knew that Gray – or his identical twin – had done the robberies.

A teller picked Gray out of a photo lineup, and we tracked him down and made the arrest. Other officers brought him to the South Portland Police Department, where I was waiting to interview him.

I took a few minutes to find out everything I could about Richard Gray, starting with his criminal history. I set the interview room up to my liking; it was a big room with nothing in it except for a big oval table and a television. On top of the television was an old cruiser video camera that we sometimes used to record interviews.

In the middle of that otherwise empty table I placed a stack of case files, three inches thick. I wanted him to see those files and think that I knew every single thing that he had done wrong, from the moment of his birth to the point where he walked into those banks a few days earlier.

What he wouldn't know is that those were just random files that I borrowed from another detective's desk.

Just a teenager, Gray arrived in the interview room looking

pretty shabby. I let him stew for a few minutes, wondering what would happen next. I walked in without looking at him, wearing my finest suit, and I must say I looked pretty good for once. My tie was tight and I projected an air of competence. He was mentally defeated before I opened my mouth.

In less than a minute Gray confessed to the robberies, explaining why he did it, how much money he got, and what he did with the cash. He did what most bank robbers should do with their spoils. He bought some marijuana, some nice bongs to smoke it with, and he gave a lot of money to his friends.

All police officers, including me, have a legal responsibility to ensure that the suspect's rights are protected, and not trampled on. We make decisions that could certainly affect the outcome of the case, and impact our own liablility. There are plenty of people willing to sue the police, and just as many attorneys happy to take their case. I can speak from experience having been the defendant in two federal court cases. Yes, I was found not guilty after two trails. I was confident the decisions made in this case were the proper ones.

I have to say this for young Richard Gray, who would eventually be sentenced to more than four years in federal prison: At least he was generous.

Chapter Twelve

Broken laws, broken people

The drug trade is a nasty business.

Whether you're a dealer or a user, the drug consumes you, takes over your life. You have no friends. You learn to snitch on your neighbor or even your brother if it will keep you out of jail and give you the chance to make more money, or to get a few more highs. The old you – the person you were before the drugs took over – isn't even a memory.

I had seen a glimpse of this during my years on patrol and then on the detective bureau. But that was nothing compared to what I would see from 2000 to 2005, when I was assigned to serve on the Maine Drug Enforcement Agency.

Some of my work for the agency would be undercover, and a lot of it would be working directly with a vast number of informants. If you want to catch big fish, you have to get help from a lot of smaller ones.

There were five or six agents there when I came on board and got a desk on the third floor of a brick building in downtown Portland. All of us were basically loaned out by our respective departments.

The task was simple: Fight the flow of illegal drugs into Cumberland County, which is Maine's most heavily populated area, with a population of about 275,000. Like most counties in Maine, Cumberland County is spread out over a large geographic area. It can take an hour to drive from Portland to the outermost towns.

The office was a wide-open floor with a few cubicles, which made it easy to shoot the shit with the other agents, or throw things at them depending on the mood of the day.

Fortunately, our administrative assistant had more patience than anyone I've ever known. She needed it. Sandy Mann was the only female in a room full of drug agents who were not opposed to swearing, farting, burping and making fun of people. Sandy, who also served in the Maine Army National Guard, could hang with the best of us – except of course for the farting and burping. Besides putting up with us, she made us look good. Sandy literally spent hours correcting my reports with a red pen so they would look presentable and sound somewhat literate before I sent them to court.

Sandy held herself to very high standards, and she accepted nothing less from those she worked with. For that, I owe her more than I could ever repay.

To begin with, I started cruising around in my state-issued Chevy Cavalier, and did some of the most important work assigned to the newest members of the task force – coffee making and errand-running.

Within a few weeks I got my first undercover assignment. Frank Stepnick, a fellow South Portland officer and a friend, told me he had an informant who could take me to buy some Oxycontin tablets from an older couple. Oxycontin and other prescription painkillers like Percocet and Vicodin were hot commodities at the time, especially in the sprawling rural areas of Maine. People like to crush the pills and snort them for a quick, powerful high. Not a week went by that we didn't hear about pharmacy robberies or home invasions where painkillers were the goal.

This elderly couple lived on the outskirts of the county and it took me and the informant about 45 minutes to get there. I had butterflies in my stomach for the whole drive. When we finally arrived at the run-down trailer, the informant told me he didn't want me to go in with him. I didn't know any better so I sent him in alone with some money. He returned a few minutes later and handed me the pills. I drove away with an entourage of surveillance vehicles following me, and it didn't take me long to complete the paperwork and send it to the court. Within a few weeks, warrants had been issued.

I drove back with a few other agents to arrest these villainous drug traffickers. What I found inside the trailer was one of the many surprises I would encounter while doing drug work. The old woman was so overweight she couldn't get off the couch. Had I been cheap enough to arrest her, she would have needed an ambulance to get her to the jail. And the husband, a sad-looking guy in his 70s, was battling cancer. They were selling his Oxy tablets to buy food and keep that trailer heated.

In the eyes of the criminal justice system, these people broke the law. In my eyes, these were broken people.

For those who sit on the sidelines, watch crime shows on television and pay taxes every year for police protection, it's easy to think of our world as a simple one, where bad people do bad things and the good guys save the day. Anyone who has ever carried a badge knows the truth. There are no simple answers.

I think that's why I excelled as a drug agent. Every case like that first one was a reality check for me. I always knew that I was one mistake away from being just like all of those addicts I arrested. That's not to say I tolerated the use of illegal drugs. I still don't. But I understand why people do it.

As a drug agent, I used the same skills of compassion and empathy that served me well on patrol and as a detective. Most addicts would talk to me because I gave them a reason to do so. I put my hand on their shoulder.

"You're a good person," I'd tell them. "You've got an addiction and you need help."

Their options were clear. Cooperate with me and I will be your best friend and advocate. Don't cooperate and you'll end up dead or in jail.

I would arrest some junkie and get him to pay off his debt to society by becoming my informant. Not too many folks told me to stuff it up my ass. I think they knew that I was being sincere and I wanted to help them out of the pit they were in. I never trusted one of them, but they trusted me.

That line of work, though, took its toll. I was working too many hours and missing too many baseball and soccer games with my kids. Even when I was there, too often my mind was somewhere else. My work was a slideshow of death, degradation and filth, and then I would return home where I was expected to be a loving husband and doting father. It wasn't easy.

The informants didn't make it easier. They have a funny way of not working. That meant it was not a problem for them to call me at 2 a.m. to give me a great scoop on a dealer, as if the guy would suddenly stop dealing in the middle of the night. When the phone rang and there was work to be done, I was out the door. I cannot be more grateful to my wife and kids for putting up with my absences, whether I was physically gone, or mentally.

One way cops deal with the stresses of the job is through black humor. That's a nice way of saying we make fun of people. The intent is not evil, it's just that we need to vent or we'll self-destruct. The stress of the job can be unbearable at times. Laughter is a tool that we use to manage that stress.

We even found ways to lighten up the mood while searching a suspect's apartment or house for drugs. I searched more properties during my years on the MDEA than most officers will do during their entire careers. Search after search, I saw the direct correlation between drugs and sex. Inevitably we would find a stash of porn and sex toys. Someone would yell, "I got it," and the rest of us would go into the room to find our colleague standing there with a big grin on his face, holding up a 12-inch vibrator.

I can only guess how many people returned home after we did our searches, only to discover a sex toy left running in the top drawer. It took so little for us to be amused, yet it meant so much at the time.

Scott Pelletier, my old friend from the police academy, became my supervisor at the MDEA soon after I joined. He is a bit of a prankster himself, so he wasn't opposed to us finding amusement during unpleasant situations. We needed that sense of humor on many occasions, like the time we gave an informant some money to buy crack.

Scott did not like to lose money, so our informant had strict instructions that he would not give the dealer the money until he had the product in hand. Some dealers had a tendency of saying, "Give me the money and I'll go get the stuff. I'll be right back." Those people had a way of disappearing.

Our informant, who had been so carefully instructed, goes ahead and gives this dealer the money up front. I think he was convinced that the dealer would come right back.

Several of us were watching from a distance, and we saw the dealer and his friend walk away. When they were several blocks down the street it was pretty clear they weren't coming back. He was ripping our informant off. This would not be acceptable to Scott or anyone else on the team.

As we made the decision to go get the cash back, I was confident of two things: We would get the money, and our informant was about to get burned. There would be no doubt in the dealer's mind that he had just been set up.

We watched the dealer and his friend walk into a parking lot at a not-so-upscale watering hole. I pulled into the lot in my stealthy Dodge Intrepid, and the dynamic duo took off running with one sight of me. I accelerated through the lot until I saw a wooden retaining wall. I stomped on the brake, skidded and stopped about six inches short of the wall. Then I jumped out and grabbed the dealer about 20 feet from my car.

I had just started to pat him down when I heard this incredible crash behind me. Before I could even turn around to see what had happened, this poor mope looked at me and said "I'm sorry."

I turned and saw that my partner, Sean Lally, had crashed his 4x4 pickup into my car. The back end of the Dodge was crumpled from the impact, and the front end of the car was smashed into that wooden retaining wall that I had been so careful to avoid. Now my trusty Dodge looked like a metal accordion.

Sean, an all around good guy and cop, had been in such a hurry that he forgot to shift his truck into park when he jumped out of the cab.

We got the money back, but this dealer didn't have any drugs on him. The only thing we found in his pockets was a set of false teeth. I love that.

Sean and I must have sounded like a couple of school boys in that parking lot, laughing our asses off and saying things like, "You better call Scott." "I'm not calling him, you call him." "You hit me, I didn't hit you, so you call."

Chapter Thirteen

Following Edward Hackett

Sept. 26, 2003
Headline: UTAH PAROLEE CHARGED WITH COLBY
KILLING Edward Hackett will answer to murder and
kidnapping charges in the death of Dawn Rossignol.

Some criminals do things that are so horrible, it can raise the goose pimples on your arms years after you deal with them.

When I think of evil, I think of Edward Hackett.

By the fall of 2003, I had become an experienced drug agent, and I loved my assignment with the Maine Drug Enforcement Agency. One of the best aspects of the job was that we had the chance to help out other law enforcement agencies around the state when they needed our expertise. In September, we got a call for help from the Maine State Police.

They were investigating the brutal murder of Dawn Rossignol, a senior at Colby College in Waterville, a small town about 75 miles north of Portland on the interstate.

The 21-year-old Rossignol had been abducted and her body was found a day after she went missing, near a stream about a mile away from the college. She had been viciously beaten and drowned. The specific details of her death are important why I feel Hackett is so evil, but out of respect for her loving family, I will leave them out.

This type of crime was unheard of in the quiet town of Waterville, and the killing made headlines throughout Maine and beyond. The media scrutiny put even more pressure on the state police to find the killer and make an arrest. Resources can get stretched real thin when you are talking about a high-profile case that is riddled with complications. Several investigators are working on multiple tasks at once, and people start to get drained. Adrenaline is a gift from God but it only lasts for so long.

I was brought into the fold to help with surveillance on a "hard target." In other words, the state police detectives were pretty sure they knew who did it, but they needed a few more pieces of evidence to make the arrest.

Conducting surveillance was a skill that I had developed quickly after becoming a drug agent. I had learned to sit in a vehicle for hours observing a target house, and to blend into traffic and follow a vehicle without being noticed.

My assignment was to watch Edward Hackett, and to follow his every movement. Hackett was on parole from a prison in Utah, where he had been incarcerated for the past 11 years for kidnapping a woman. At the time of the Rossignol murder, he was living with his mother in Vassalboro, another small town in central Maine, just south of Waterville.

In this case, I would call my job 'following,' instead of surveillance. It was impossible to conduct moving surveillance without being noticed in a town with only a handful of residents and fewer paved roads.

Hackett knew he was a suspect. State Police detectives had spoken with every sex offender in the area, and Hackett's criminal history in Utah – plus some of the strange answers he gave to detectives – put a big red flag on his name.

The rumor mill in Vassalboro must have been operating in high gear, as unmarked police cars cruised in and out of town regularly. Not to mention the small army of vehicles parked near Hackett's house.

On my second day of that assignment, Hackett was on the move, and I was among the motorcade of cops that tailed him to Augusta, the state capitol. We were told not to lose him, and there was no way that was going to happen. Just outside of Augusta, Hackett pulled into a convenience store. It was the first time I got a good look at him. He stood over six feet tall and reminded me of a woodsman. Not obviously muscular, but he could probably pick up a vehicle if he had to.

Hackett's trunk wasn't shut tightly, so I mentioned it to him when he came out of the store. I had nothing to lose, so I figured what the hell, maybe he'll like me. Hackett looked at me and thanked me after he closed the trunk. It was the beginning of our short-lived friendship. He was kind enough to tell me he was headed to his doctor's office. Apparently he didn't want us to lose him in traffic.

One of the other agents updated state police officials, and we were told that Hackett was probably headed to the Augusta Mental Health Institute, the state-run psychiatric facility. The place has since been renamed with a much more pleasant-sounding title, Riverview Psychiatric Center.

I wasn't happy about heading to AMHI. Some people have an aversion to snakes or spiders. I have a fear of psychiatric hospitals. I just can't shake that vision of Jack Nicholson in One Flew Over the Cuckoo's Nest.

The campus at AMHI reminded me of an old, unkempt college campus, with looming brick buildings that needed repairs.

Agent Stacy Blair and I were told to follow Hackett on the grounds. He was not under arrest and we couldn't interfere with his movements, but the state police brass wanted to keep the pressure on him. I slid my cassette recorder into my coat pocket as I parked next to Hackett. He had been kind enough to tell me where he was going, so I told him that Stacy and I would be walking with him for a while. He took the news well and sort of grunted.

Hackett knew his way around and was clearly a familiar face at the hospital. One woman approached him and greeted him warmly.

"How are you doing?" she asked him.

"I've been a bad boy," he responded in a creepy childish voice.

That brought to mind another classic Jack Nicholson character, the demented innkeeper in The Shining. I started to sweat.

Hackett made himself at home. At one point, he curled up on

the floor of an office. A doctor walked into the office and came back out a few minutes later. He asked us if we were there for Hackett, and Stacy and I explained our mission. The doctor pressed us. He said he wanted Hackett out of his office. I wish I knew what Hackett said in there. It's not a good sign when the doctor you go to for help wants you kicked out.

Soon afterward, Hackett opened the door and walked downstairs and back outside with Stacy and I close behind. We all sat down at a picnic table. It was obvious that he was exhausted. I didn't want him to rest, so I kept talking to him.

Slowly, Hackett rose and walked into another building. He spoke to a receptionist briefly and then went into a bathroom. There was a loud noise, and when I opened the bathroom door I saw Hackett lying on his ass. He had thrown up and fallen on the floor. As I helped him up I had a thought.

"You look like crap," I told Hackett. "You should let me drive you home."

I tend to be a methodical and calculated person when it comes to investigating a case, but I can also be very impulsive at times.

Why in hell would I offer to give a suspected murderer a ride in my car, knowing damn well his house wasn't right around the corner? It was either a flash of brilliant police work, or sheer stupidity.

Hackett graciously accepted the offer and we walked back to the cars. I guided him into my front seat, all the while hoping that my tape recorder would capture the confession that everyone needed to hear.

During the drive from Augusta to his mother's house in Vassalboro, Hackett maintained a thousand-mile stare, and I tried to lighten the mood with small talk and jokes. That didn't work. This guy had the sense of humor of a rattlesnake. Other cops were following us, but I didn't even notice them in the rear-view mirror. I was probably too busy wondering if this lunatic was going to kill me. It didn't help that, as usual, I had left my gun and my vest in the trunk. This was a mistake and I knew it.

I puckered a bit more when I received a call telling me to

bring Hackett to the fire station in Vassalboro, which was a mile beyond his mother's house.

As we drove past the spot where he expected to get dropped off, Hackett didn't get upset, but he did ask me where I was taking him.

"I have to go to the bathroom," I said. It was all I could think of. Great undercover officers have a knack for thinking quickly on their feet. At that moment I would have been happy to be marginal rather than great. I wanted him out of my car.

I wouldn't say I was afraid of Hackett, but he certainly gave me the creeps. He appeared to have no human emotions; at least none that I detected.

State Police Detective Joe Zamboni came outside the fire station and asked Hackett if he could speak with him for a minute. Joe had already interviewed Hackett once, and was hoping to close the deal with a confession. I waited in the open bay, admiring the fire trucks.

Five minutes passed before Joe came out searching for a mop. Hackett was still maintaining his innocence in the Rossignol killing, but just as he stood up to leave he vomited all over himself and the floor. That is a picture of stress at its finest.

Hackett walked outside and laid down on the grassy lawn.

Joe Zamboni decided to give it one more shot to get a confession, but gave up after a few minutes. In my time with Hackett, I had seen no soul behind his eyes – only an unfeeling coldness. I figured Joe was getting that same feeling as he walked back toward the fire station. He had a look of frustration on his face that I was way too familiar with.

I asked Joe I could take a run at Hackett. I had spent some time with him that day, and I thought he might give it up. Joe told me to go ahead.

The smell – a dreadful combination of body odor and vomit – was the first thing I noticed when I approached Hackett on the lawn. Hackett was lying on his side, so I walked behind him and got down on one knee.

In a gentle, calming voice I methodically explained his options.

He would feel much better, I told him, if he would get everything off his chest. I even threw in the old standby: "Bad people do bad things and good people do bad things," suggesting that he was a decent guy who made a mistake.

It was my best stuff, but he was just lying there.

My leg started to cramp up, so I stood and walked around to the front of him. I was starting to seriously doubt my interviewing skills, until I saw his face. That son of a bitch was sound asleep.

Here it was, my one moment to shine and leave my mark on the field of law enforcement forever, and the prick slept through it all. So much for my moment.

Later that afternoon, detectives spread the word: Hackett's DNA had been found under one of the door handles of Rossignol's car. They arrested Hackett and he eventually confessed not only to police but to a reporter from the Portland Press Herald. Hackett even told the reporter that he should never be let out of jail.

Don't worry, Edward, that won't happen.

On March 19, 2004, Superior Court Justice Donald Marden sentenced the 47-year-old Hackett to life in prison. Because Maine has no parole, the sentence means Hackett will never be released.

Chapter Fourteen

One picture is worth 1,000 words

I didn't know what to expect as we made our way down Pearl Lane, a quiet street in Chamblee, Georgia.

It was the last known address for Thong Nguyen. From my discussion with Sang Tran, I believed that Thong Nguyen might hold the keys to the entire robbery case. We had to find him and figure out if we were headed in the right direction.

If I ever lost focus, all I had to do was to think about the look on little Alex Tran's face after those thugs had tied her and her cousin up.

Captain David Perkins of the Chamblee Police Department was kind enough to be our tour guide, but I got the impression that he looked at us like foreigners. We didn't talk like him, nor did we have that Georgia tan he was accustomed to. I looked like the really pale white guy from Maine that I was.

The five-minute tour of Asian Square had been impressive. It made the Maine Mall look like a convenience store. I had never seen so many restaurants, shops, nail salons and specialty stores, and all of them were filled with people. I'm a big fan of Chinese food, but the smell of fried rice and dumplings was almost overpowering.

When we got to Pearl Lane, I noticed that the houses were only a few feet apart from one another, with just enough room to store some broken lawn mowers and trash. We still have places in Maine where you can't build a house unless you own five acres.

We found the place where Thong Nguyen supposedly was living, but of course he wasn't there. If I had a dime for every person I went looking for, only to come up empty, I'd be a very wealthy man. We walked around a bit and it didn't take me long to figure out that I was a minority in this particular subdivision, and I might as well have had "COP" written across my forehead. Captain Perkins reminded me not to get my hopes up.

Some people, though, did speak with us. The bad news was that Thong Nguyen didn't live on Pearl Lane anymore. The good news was that neighbors knew his latest address – the Dekalb County Jail.

I really needed a picture of Thong Nguyen and a records check. I got more than I ever expected through the help of the folks at the Gwinnett County Sheriff's Department. That was the agency that had arrested Nguyen just a few weeks earlier for assault. Turns out Nguyen was being held at the jail at the request of federal immigration officers.

The record system at Gwinnett County was nothing short of amazing. They gave Mike Saenz and I enough reports to make our head spin.

Finally, I saw the photograph of Thong Nguyen that was taken after his most recent arrest. I took one look at the photo and knew. This was one of our guys.

Alex had described one of the robbers as an older man with a mole on the side of his face. There was Thong Nguyen, with a huge mole on his face. He was in his mid-30s but looked many years older.

A detective was kind enough to compile all the reports on Thong Nguyen, as well as booking photos of people he had been arrested with. There were evidence photos attached to one of the cases, including a Polaroid of a white Oldsmobile that was used in the commission of a crime.

I remembered the teenagers back in Scarborough telling me that an older Asian man had arrived at Kieu's house in North Carolina in a white vehicle. The car broke down while the group of men was there. I looked at the photograph of the Oldsmobile and figured I could prove that he owned the car at the time of the robbery. I was thinking to myself, 'Shit, this is like real detective work.' My confidence was growing.

I carried our stack of paperwork back to the hotel that evening, and spent a few hours studying every detail, like a college student getting ready for a final. I didn't want to miss anything that could help me if I got the chance to interview Thong Nguyen in jail. I memorized the faces and ages of his associates, learned if they had children and jobs, anything that I might need for leverage in the future. This painstaking work never makes its way into the one-hour police dramas you see on television.

At the point where my mind shut down and refused to take in any more new information, I called home to check on my wife and kids, then decided that a nice cold beer would fix what was ailing me. Mike was all for it, and we set out on foot.

It was just after midnight and to our surprise we had a hard time finding a watering hole. The weather was colder than I had expected, and of course I had packed like a guy, too light. Eventually we spotted some people milling around a business that had a neon sign in the front window. I did what cops do and found a table that had a view to the door, and I sat with my back to the wall.

I couldn't help but notice that our waiter was skipping more than he was walking. This wasn't a problem as long as he could deliver the goods, and by that I mean a cold draft beer. Mike ordered the special, a chili dog with fries.

The clues then started to fall into place about our chosen establishment. There were no women. One gentleman at the bar had his arm around the gentleman next to him. I subtly pointed out my amazing detective work to Mike, and we realized that we were two cops from Maine, sitting smack dab in the middle of a gay bar in Atlanta.

Now don't get me wrong. I'm no homophobe. Some friends of mine – and some of the best witnesses that ever took the stand – have been gay. But I just didn't feel comfortable going to the bathroom in a gay bar. I was too far from home and really didn't know where I was in Atlanta. I really had to go. Mike told me he had my back, but that brought me little reassurance.

So I held it. I waited patiently for my beer, which went down

Kieu Nguyen

Cong Nguyen

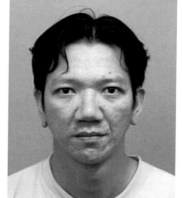

Quyen Le

Thong Nguyen

Nam Nguyen

Tran home after the burglary.

Note the tape, and video cord on the bed
used to restrain the girls.

Photo of Edward Hackett at the time of his arrest
for killing Dawn Rossignol.

Martinez, Juan Joseph

Renardo Williams
Note the name he gave the jail employees.

Nine pounds of cocaine, $138,000 in cash, and
several handguns that were seized.

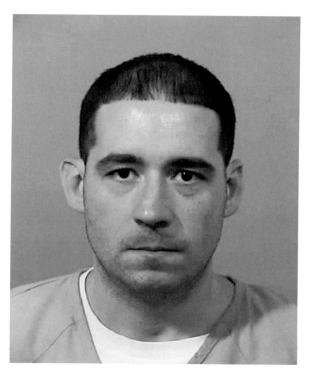

Patrick Dorney

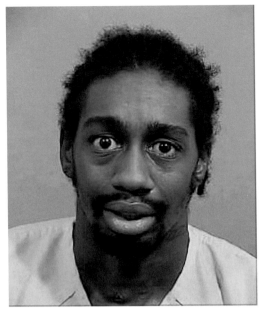

Terrel Dubois

The spot where Steve Connors
was ambushed and shot.

L to R: MDEA Director Roy McKinney, SPPD Chief Ed Googins, and me at an MDEA recognition ceremony in 2006.

L to R: ADA Bud Ellis, AAG Lea-Anne Sutton, Cumberland County District Attorney Stephanie Anderson and me.

as smooth as water, and then I waited for Mike to finish his meal. I suffered through the walk back to the hotel, where I used my bathroom in privacy.

It had been one of the most productive days in my investigation of the Tran robbery, and I will be forever grateful to Mike Saenz for sharing some great laughs to top it all off.

I knew that some good humor would serve me well as I prepared for my next task – the most important interview of my career.

Chapter Fifteen

You can't pick your victims

On a cold November morning in 2003, my son and I were supposed to be raking leaves for a family in need. Instead, I ended up chasing after a drug dealer named Pedro Santiago.

Scott Durst was a fellow police officer who had been sent to fight in Iraq with his Army reserve unit. His family lived in the rural community of Buxton, about a half-hour west of Portland. A large crew of friends met up at the Durst house one morning to rake leaves and do other odd jobs. It was the least we could do while Scott was overseas serving our country.

My boss at the Maine Drug Enforcement Agency, Scott Pelletier, and another drug agent, Kevin Cashman, were part of the group that arrived with rakes.

Scott got a phone call around 10 a.m. Portland detectives wanted help with a shooting that had just happened, and it was apparently drug related. Scott sent me and Kevin, who was on loan to the agency from the Portland Police Department. He had just started his stint as a drug agent, so he didn't have a clue what he was doing.

Kevin is a white man with an afro, and he was a hell of a baseball player in college. He was about to get a couple of valuable lessons and to his credit, he was more than happy to learn them.

I left my son with Scott, and Kevin and I drove to Portland. Other officers filled us in on the case.

Josh Dyer was a 20-year-old with drug problems. He had apparently ripped off a local dealer, Pedro Santiago, on the night of Nov. 7, and Santiago took exception. In the morning, Santiago showed up at Dyer's apartment and shot him in the head.

Dyer was as good as dead, but doctors were still having talks with his family members about whether he would donate his organs. Several witnesses saw the shooting but most of them were not talking to police. As for Santiago, he was gone.

Kevin and I researched reports on Dyer and Santiago, and we helped out with some phone records. You always have to be careful not to be too pushy when you are helping out another department; some officers don't like outsiders pushing their noses in too deep. I've always considered it an honor and compliment to be asked to help, but I also know there's a big difference between helping and trying to take over a case.

I told the lieutenant of the Portland detective bureau that I would do whatever he asked. He mentioned the names of some of the supposed witnesses, and asked if Kevin and I could track them down. I was familiar with some of the names, and I had a hunch they would be holding vigil somewhere in the hospital where their friend was dying. The hunch was right, and before long we were talking to people who had been in the apartment when the fatal shot was fired.

One of the people, a girl, had information about the case and I had a feeling she was lying to us. I called one of the detectives on the case and asked him to pick her up and bring her to police headquarters. It's a lot easier to lie when you are surrounded by friends than it is when you are sitting in a police interview room. The detective picked her up and obtained a helpful statement from the girl.

Kevin and I returned to the Portland Police Department later that afternoon, and the scene sort of shocked me. Earlier there had been several detectives around, including two supervisors. But there were only two detectives at the office when we came back. This was about to be a homicide and the most important work is done in the hours after the crime is committed. I couldn't believe it when I was told that everyone else had gone home. There was so much work to be done, but who was going to do it?

Kevin Cashman and I refused to leave at that point. We worked closely with the two remaining detectives to piece together a sequence of events.

Dyer and a friend had met up with Santiago the night before to buy cocaine. Dyer got the drugs, but then threw some money at Santiago. It wasn't enough. Pissed at having been ripped off, Santiago drove after Dyer and actually ran into their car, causing some damage before Dyer got away.

We located that vehicle and Dyer's friend. The other detectives worked to track Santiago down by tracing his cell phone calls.

Word was spreading fast about the shooting, which had become a murder by the end of the day, as Dyer was pronounced dead. Inmates at the jail in Portland watched the story on the 6 o'clock news. Shortly after 8 p.m. I got a call from a corrections officer. One of the inmates that I had arrested had some information for me. I had been decent to her and she was about to repay the favor. She told me that Santiago was hiding in the City of Biddeford, a short drive to the south of Portland.

We learned that there were two locations where Santiago might be hiding out. I looked at Kevin and asked him what he thought.

"Let's go," he said without hesitating.

The other detectives weren't sure if the tip was worth pursuing. I politely told them that they could do whatever they wanted. We were going to find Santiago. To their credit, they saw the case through as we did.

Kevin and I stopped at the Biddeford Police Department to let them know what we were doing, and they were quite accommodating. Like many blue-collar towns scattered around New England, Biddeford was a once thriving mill town that had fallen on hard times. Drug use and violence were the norm for the row houses downtown.

It didn't take long before we spotted the pickup truck we were looking for. It was parked on a street about a block from one of the apartments where we expected to find our man. This apparently got the juices flowing again back in Portland because we were told to stay put. Some Portland detectives and supervisors were on their way.

It seemed like hours, but it was really only about 30 minutes before we got the green light to go to the apartment on our street. We were joined by some burly Biddeford officers who were more than willing to help. I took a position at the rear of the apartment, in case Santiago jumped out a window. At the front door, Kevin made contact with someone inside, but she refused to open the door.

All of a sudden we were all told over the radio to abandon our posts and get over to the second location as soon as possible.

I couldn't believe it. They were going to let this guy get away. I did a lot of bitching to Kevin in the two minutes it took us to drive to the second apartment. When we got there I saw police cars, marked and unmarked, clogging the entire road. I saw Sgt. Tom Joyce, a man whom I admired greatly for his investigative skills.

The resident of the apartment had just come out and told police that Santiago was inside. That was why they had us leave the other apartment. It wasn't long before Santiago was escorted outside in handcuffs.

I had a sense of relief and accomplishment. Kevin and I didn't give up and we chose not to let the social status of the victim, Josh Dyer, dictate our decisions. For the longest time I felt that more effort should have been put forth that day by the Portland Police Department. I had a long conversation with Kevin about the importance of following every lead, no matter how small, and I stressed to him that you treat every victim as a victim. You cannot pick your victims, and you should never judge them.

Years later, I talked to Sgt. Tom Joyce about that case, and how it bothered me that only two detectives stayed on the job that night. He made me realize that there weren't just two detectives, there were four. I never really counted myself or Kevin into the mix. Tom knew that we were there, and he knew about my work ethic because of cases we had worked on together in the past. He had faith in the skeleton crew that was tracking Santiago that night, and he believed that if anyone could find him, it was us.

Santiago went to trial and was found guilty of the murder of Joshua Dyer, a father and a son. Santiago was sentenced to 40 years in prison.

All this for $200 worth of cocaine.

Chapter Sixteen

When nobodies lead to somebodies

Working drug cases is never monotonous. Some of the people I've arrested made me laugh my ass off. Others pissed me off to no end.

The variety and spice of life that I experienced while working at the Maine Drug Enforcement Agency, no doubt, kept me going when my body felt like shutting down. I have seen the good, the bad and the ugly. Guys who watched their teeth rot out as a result of long-term methadone use. Women who simply gave up on basic hygiene because they were too focused on their next hits.

There were days when I asked myself why I was shoveling shit upstream, busting my ass for junkies who never seemed to get better. I would arrest them and try to help them, only to arrest them a week later for doing the same thing in a different apartment.

My faith and commitment to stomping out drugs wavered on more than one occasion, but there were also events that recharged my battery for a while.

The first week of January in 2004, me and the other guys at MDEA were having a good time because our friend and fearless leader, Scott Pelletier was out of work. He had taken a nasty fall while hanging up Christmas lights at his house. Oh yeah, he was standing on a small stepladder when he fell from a staggering height of about two feet. His arm was busted up bad enough to need surgery.

I always told Scott he was an accident waiting to happen, and it finally happened. Drug agents, of course, are trained to think on their feet and function at a high level without much supervision, so being without Scott for a few weeks wasn't much of a challenge. In other words, we had a great time.

On the evening of January 4th, though, we were about to hit a lucky streak.

The staff at one of the hotels in South Portland called to complain about possible drug use in one of their rooms. The classic signs were there: too many visitors to the room, lots of phone calls to local numbers, and the renter had paid in cash.

When we arrived, we found a group of people from Portland who had come across the bridge to smoke some crack in peace. The room itself yielded very little evidence, just some crack pipes and some residue. We cleared the room out and didn't waste our time arresting anyone because it wouldn't be worth the time it took to fill out the paperwork. On the overall picture of the drug trade, these were nobodies.

But there was one guy who stood out. He was sweating profusely, and it certainly was not hot outside that hotel in January. Turns out this guy had a receipt from a stolen ATM card in his pocket. He also had a string of felony convictions for theft, and one more would send him back to prison. That would motivate most people. In the parking lot, he told me that he would be willing to help me out in order to remain a free man.

Being a simple man, I had a simple request. Buy drugs for me.

We reached a gentleman's agreement that he would buy cocaine from a supplier the following night, and I wouldn't charge him with the ATM card theft. I couldn't lose with this one. I could always arrest him later if he stiffed me.

On January 5th there was a lot of chatter in the office. We were debating the odds that this guy would actually come through. I didn't like my chances, but sure enough, the guy called us, just as he was instructed.

This dude had little pride left because he agreed to buy cocaine from his own cousin. Hell, we didn't care.

We wired him up, gave him some money and it was game on.

It was to be a simple buy and walk. Nobody was going to jail that day. We wanted leverage on the cousin so we could pick him up another day and get him to flip, too. That's how you get the major players. You have to move up and up the food chain.

The buy went down in a congested area of Portland, so we had a few of the other agents help with surveillance. Pat Lally worked for the Westbrook Police Department and had been assigned to MDEA for a few months. His brother Sean was the guy who wrecked my car in a parking lot during a deal. Scott Durst was the supervisor while Pelletier was nursing his broken arm. Durst had recently returned to Maine from Iraq, where he had spent too many months with his Army reserve unit. He wasn't crazy, but he was well on his way. He's a great friend, so I can get away with saying that. Good old Kevin Cashman was still around from the Portland Police Department, and he was still quite the jokester.

Everything went smooth as silk. Our informant met up with his cousin near Congress Street and handed him some money. Cousin told him he would be right back with the cocaine. As usual, cousin was essentially a middle-man. He didn't want our informant to know where he was going to get the product.

Here's how it works. A gives money to B to purchase cocaine for him. Let's say $100 cash. B goes to C, his supplier, and says he needs a gram of crack. As long as B is a good customer and a frequent flier, the dealer will sell him the gram for $90, so B can make a few bucks for himself. B returns to A and hands him the crack he just bought, with a sliver taken off for his own use. A is happy because he can get high again; B is happy because he made $10 and he too can smoke up. The supplier is the happiest. He just sold a gram of crack for $90, when he probably bought it wholesale for $20.

Our surveillance team watched the informant's cousin as he walked through the side streets and alleys of Portland. Finally, he entered an apartment on Brackett Street, about 25 feet from one of the city's largest elementary schools. We had received intelligence for a while about this apartment, but we had never gotten anyone inside. Other informants had told me that the guys who lived there sold large quantities of cocaine, and at least one of them had a gun inside.

Sometimes things just come together. We tried and failed for months to get into this place. Then, one overweight thief who likes to steal and smoke crack unwittingly gets us in by setting up his own cousin.

I spent what seemed like hours on the phone with the prosecutor, Lea-Anne Sutton of the Maine Attorney General's Office. I was convinced that we had enough credible information to obtain an unannounced entry search warrant, which would allow us to use the Portland Police Department's Special Reaction Team, and really rock the world of the men inside that apartment.

Lea-Anne and I have always had an incredible amount of mutual respect, but this was one of those rare occasions when we disagreed. She must have gotten sick of my whining, though, and she agreed that we probably had enough to get the type of warrant we wanted.

A judge signed off on the warrant just before midnight. The plan was to let the team make entry, and we would go in afterward and clean up the mess. This technique was much safer for us, so I'm sure my wife appreciated that decision.

I heard the flash bangs go off and people hollering. After a few minutes, I walked toward the apartment building and up the steps like I owned the place. The SRT members brought out two men.

We let them stew for a few minutes, as we went to search the apartment. The smell was terrible. It was an odd mixture of flash bang residue and a smoldering mattress that momentarily caught on fire in the bedroom.

There was a loaded handgun on the bedroom floor, and two more in the living room. Within a few minutes we found two ounces of cocaine, two ounces of crack and about $17,000 in cash. Busts of that size might be common in the large metropolitan areas, but this was a good grab for Portland. Those guys waiting out in the police car were players, and now they had a huge incentive to talk to us.

One of them knew that he was screwed, so he decided his best option was to cooperate and join Team America, if you will. He agreed to call his source of supply the next morning and order up some cocaine.

By 7 a.m., myself and another agent were at the jail and taking this guy outside in his orange jumpsuit. He said all he knew about the source was his cell phone number. We asked him if it would be crazy to order a kilo – 2.2 pounds. We almost shit when he said that wouldn't be crazy at all. We prayed that the source had not seen any of the media coverage of the raid on Brackett Street.

Our informant made the call and his source never flinched when he ordered the kilo. The source agreed to meet our guy at the apartment in an hour. We needed the informant to point him out, so we all drove to Brackett Street and sat in the car.

We had several other officers waiting inside the apartment.

"That's him," our informant said.

I had been distracted for a moment.

"That's who?" I mumbled. Sure enough, we picked the wrong parking spot, because the source was walking up behind us, headed for the apartment. I didn't breathe for a full minute. Luckily for me he walked right on by.

I saw some flying elbows at the door, and the next thing I knew our guy was in handcuffs. We recovered a kilo of cocaine, and another kilo in the rental car he was driving.

There was no way to lose with the interview. He was caught with a kilo of cocaine in hand, and he knew it was done. We slid past the Miranda issue and in a personable manner he told me his name was Juan Martinez.

I let him stick with that for a while, even though I knew he was bullshitting me. This guy was a black male, and in no way was he Hispanic. He claimed that he was from New Jersey and had been selling cocaine in Maine for about six months. I wasn't hearing any accent.

Before shipping Mr. Martinez off to jail, I told him he was full of shit. He was quiet and soft spoken and just grinned at me when I told him that.

I made yet another gentleman's agreement that day. If he turned out to be Juan Martinez, I would drive to whatever jail he was in, shake his hand and apologize. But if his name was not Juan Martinez, he would have to apologize to me.

Based on all the information we had gathered, we were able to conduct several more searches throughout Portland. This was the kind of big case that I had been waiting for years to break. When we finally wrapped up the loose ends and held a press conference, we had approximately nine pounds of cocaine on display, and almost $140,000 in cash.

Just before the press conference I got even more good news. My friend Juan Martinez was actually Renardo Williams of Boston.

Renardo had a decent reason to lie to me. He was wanted for two homicides and a third attempted homicide in Boston in 2003. No wonder he came to Maine.

He was ultimately found not guilty for the killings in Massachusetts, but he couldn't escape punishment for his drug dealing in Portland. Williams was sentenced to 16 years in prison.

The last time I spoke to Renardo was at the jail in Portland. I have to give the man credit. He shook my hand and said he was sorry.

Chapter Seventeen

"She remembers you"

Finding Thong Nguyen was a combination of hard work and sheer luck.

Interviewing him would only require one skill. I simply could not flinch. I had not come all this way seeking justice for Alex Tran, only to blow it with one poorly phrased question or a clumsy gesture that Thong might take offense at.

There was way too much testosterone in the room, from the crowd of men who had assembled to watch the interview inside the Dekalb County Jail. It was not the ideal situation, but this was their place and frankly I didn't dare to tell them what to do.

To preserve the element of surprise, no one told Thong we were coming to speak with him, and of course he had no idea that I had been waiting months for this day.

Thong was supposed to have been deported already, but he was originally from Vietnam, and that country was not taking convicts back from the U.S. He was basically being held in Georgia until he was shipped to another federal holding facility in another state. Because his immigration status was in limbo, he would likely be released soon.

The interview room had brick walls and a concrete floor.

Thong Nguyen was sitting straight up and he looked right at me, as if he knew that I was the one who wanted to speak with him, before anyone said a word.

Looking at Thong, dressed in his jail garb, with pale skin and pain in his eyes, I could tell that his life had been hard. He had no confidence in himself. I glanced at the feature that I knew was going to sink him, the mole on his face.

Officer Robinson Tieu of Gwinnett County Officer spoke fluent Vietnamese, so he translated. I had no idea how much English Thong could speak, but I certainly didn't want our chat ruled inadmissible in court. Officer Tieu pulled out a card that had the Miranda rights written in both languages.

I wasn't nervous. Going in, I thought that if I could get Thong through the Miranda warning and get him talking, I would get a confession. I not only knew this case, I had every little detail committed to memory.

I stared at Thong as officer Tieu read every single one of his rights. Thong not only acknowledged his rights, he agreed to speak with me.

I paused for just a moment because I wanted to speak clearly and I wanted to start the interview off with a bang. I wanted to leave no doubt in Thong's mind that I had him dead to rights. I introduced myself and told Thong that I had traveled from Maine to Atlanta just to speak with him. He showed little emotion. He said he would have no idea why I would want to speak with him.

Thong appeared to understand English well.

Shuffling slowly through my papers, I pulled out the one thing I felt might jog his memory. I put a photograph of Alex Tran on the table.

"Do you remember her?" I asked, and then continued before he could respond, "She remembers you."

"It was the mole on your face that did you in, Thong. I promised this little girl that I wouldn't stop until I caught the men that terrorized her."

Thong Nguyen looked at the table briefly. Then he nodded his head up and down.

I finally had him.

It had taken many months of slow investigative work, and the help of Mike and several others along the way, but I had him.

What happened next was almost as surprising as the speed at which Thong folded. He gave a written confession that spelled out the entire plot and the chain of events leading up to the robbery. He seemed to be remorseful for what he had done.

Thong and his friends had driven from Atlanta to North Carolina, and then to Maine. He told us that it was Kieu Minh Nguyen, also known as "Q", who came up with the idea and financed the trip. Kieu was romantically involved with Paula, Monica Tran's sister-in-law. He had also worked in the nail salon in South Portland.

Kieu told Thong and his friends that Don and Monica Tran had a significant stash of cash in their apartment.

Thong and I started to hit it off during the interview. I had brought him down at the start, and now I was building him up with words of praise and kindness. I knew there were still other robbers to identify.

I reached again into my papers and pulled out the mug shots that I had received from the officers at Gwinnett County. They were photos of every person who had been arrested with or associated with Thong Nguyen. I had just laid out the last of the photos when he started pointing at them.

One by one he identified the men who had committed the robbery with him. Cong Nguyen, Quyea Le, and Nam Nguyen. He told me about each man and their involvement in the robbery.

I left Thong Nguyen on good terms and told him that someone would be in touch with him to let him know what was happening with the case. I was thinking that this man, and hopefully three others, would soon be in Maine to face charges for what they had done to two precious girls in June of 1998.

I was elated. Mike and I had accomplished more in a few days that I had been able to accomplish in several months. Mike congratulated me and I couldn't thank him enough for getting us to Georgia.

We had just wrapped up a very important step in the criminal justice process. We had located one of the robbers and obtained a confession. But I had to keep my emotions in check. It was really only the first step. In no way did this mean that my job was done. I still had a lot of work to do if I was going to find true justice for Alex.

Back at the hotel, the first call I made was to Jon Chapman, the assistant U.S. Attorney for Maine who was my boss at the Violent Crimes Task Force. I tried to sound calm but it didn't work. Jon had faith in my abilities, but I don't think he ever thought we would actually solve this case. He too passed on his congratulations.

The second call I made was to Monica Tran.

"I got him," was all I could say when she answered the phone. She was crying by the time we hung up.

We all have good days and bad days, and this was one of the best.

Less than a week earlier I couldn't wait for the plane to land in Atlanta so I could try to make something happen with this case. Now I only wanted to get home, so the system of justice that I believed in so much could start doing its part and help me keep my promise to Alex.

Chapter Eighteen

Lessons in mortality

"It's a shallow life that doesn't give a person a few scars." –
Garrison Keillor

A methamphetamine lab can be so small, it can fit in the trunk
of a car.

The "cooker" can get all the ingredients he needs at any big
chain store. The process of manufacturing methamphetamine is
fairly simple for someone with a little know-how, the right
ingredients and a heat source. The ingredients to this little
chowder, however, are extremely combustible and potentially
toxic.

This highly addictive drug, known as meth, crystal meth or
ice, has swept across the country in recent years, destroying
countless lives along the way.

Meth addicts are often referred to as tweakers because they
tend to twitch uncontrollably when under its influence. They
also develop sores on their faces and bodies, which they pick at
constantly. Once under the spell of meth, a person begins a
downward spiral that accelerates rapidly. They look terrible, they
lose weight and their life turns into a living hell that is nearly
impossible to escape.

Addicts often smoke meth just like crack cocaine. What follows
is an intense high, which usually includes a dash of paranoia
and violence mixed in for good measure. Several documentaries
on this demon drug have been aired on television, but I usually
changed the channel when I stumbled onto one of those.

Meth really hadn't arrived in Maine, so it didn't affect my life
as a police officer. I was quite content and quite busy dealing

with my heroin addicts, crack smokers and marijuana gardeners, as I liked to call them.

The few meth labs that I had encountered in Maine had been assembled by imports – people from far-away states who had brought their manufacturing knowledge and their addictions with them. I had little knowledge about the drug, nor did I really want to learn, until July of 2004.

One day that month I was sent to speak with a woman in Gorham, a quiet bedroom community near Portland. She had been separated from her husband for about two weeks, and earlier that day she went to his house to pick up some things for their son. She had moved out because of her husband's drug use. The woman said the house had a strange odor inside, and she was concerned.

The odor, reminiscent of cat urine, combined with her husband's history of drug use and his strange behavior, suggested I was dealing with a clandestine methamphetamine laboratory, commonly called a clan lab in law enforcement circles. The family didn't have a cat.

I called Kevin Cashman, the Maine Drug Enforcement Agency's resident expert on clan labs, and he agreed with the assessment. Kevin helped me draft an application for a search warrant, which was very helpful because I couldn't even pronounce some of the chemical compounds we would be looking for, let alone spell them correctly.

It was after midnight and a rainstorm was brewing as we drove up to the house. Clouds and rain don't bother me, but lightning is not one of my favorite things. The rain came first and the lightning bolts followed. I elected to sit in my dry vehicle, which had four rubber tires, as Kevin and another agent walked into the house.

Nobody was home, so I thought it was strange when they walked back outside as quickly as they went in. Kevin had found some evidence in a trash can, and he wanted to get it outside. Just as he set it down a big puff of smoke shot up from the can. That was a pretty good clue that some nasty chemicals were in there. Discretion being the better part of valor, the boys opened up some windows to ventilate the house, then they walked outside again.

Like most states, Maine has a special team that is trained and equipped to respond to dangerous clan labs. But because the members are spread out across the state, it can take a few hours to get people mobilized and coordinated at the scene. We decided to call them in.

The homeowner returned while we were all waiting. He admitted that an acquaintance of his, Richard Cook, had been staying at the home and cooking the meth. The homeowner said he kicked Cook and another man out of the home earlier that day because of the strong odor. He said Cook loaded up his chemicals in a Dodge pickup, and then took off. That meant that Richard Cook was driving around somewhere with a potentially explosive situation on board.

An attempt to locate, or ATL, was sent to the police departments in the area. If anyone found Cook, they were supposed to detain him until MDEA agents arrived.

By that point I had already worked an extremely long day, so my supervisor Scott Pelletier told me to go home. I offered no resistance and headed home, expecting to return in the morning to watch the guys in chemical-resistant suits do their thing. Scott stayed at the scene.

I made it to my house and to the edge of my bed before the phone rang. An officer had stopped Cook's truck on Congress Street in Portland. They were waiting for me. So at 4 a.m. I put on my dirty clothes and headed back out.

I saw blue lights flashing in the distance as I approached the scene. Two uniformed officers were speaking with Cook as I parked my car.

My first mistake was one that I made too often. I left my gun in the trunk. My second mistake was not taking into account the gravity of the situation before I approached Cook. I should have known that Richard Cook would be irrational. He was a tweaker. I should also have remembered that one year earlier, Cook had lost his infant son, who had overdosed after eating some of Cook's prescription medications. These two factors were not a good combination, but my confidence and my state of exhaustion got the best of me that morning.

Cook was stoic as I introduced myself and told him I wanted to ask him a few questions. The cold, lifeless stare that I received back should have been an indication of things to come, but I still wasn't in tune with my senses, probably because of sleep deprivation.

I did most of the talking as I explained to Cook that I just wanted to get the chemicals off the street so no one would get hurt. He just looked at me. Cook was wearing a baggy sweatshirt with pockets, and he kept both hands in them the entire time that I was just inches away from him.

The conversation was one-sided, so I tried to draw something out of him. I told Cook I was sorry about what had happened to his son, and that I wasn't trying to make things worse for him. Then I asked him if he was carrying anything illegal. He looked down and told me that he wasn't.

I asked if he would mind if I searched him.

"You're not going to search me," he said.

As I was explaining to Cook that I was going to search him anyway, he hollered something that I heard as, "I can't take this." Then he turned to run.

I did what any other officer would have done, I grabbed him. This was where my instincts, fortunately, kicked back in. I noticed that Cook was curving his body back into mine, so instead of pulling him toward me I pushed his left arm away with my left hand. I can't explain what I felt or why I felt it, but something just wasn't right.

I heard a popping sound, like a firecracker.

The next thing I saw was Richard Cook lying on the sidewalk, a puddle of blood forming around his head.

My mind raced, but the thoughts were a jumble. I heard the officers saying, "shots fired" into their radios, but I never looked up. I walked a few steps away from the body and sat on a concrete windowsill.

My supervisor, Scott Pelletier, heard the radio traffic. He called my cell phone to make sure I wasn't hurt, but I wasn't in the mood for talking.

I cupped my head in my hands, oblivious to the activity around me. It was as if the lights were on, but nobody was home. Sirens wailed as the firemen, rescue personnel, and additional police officers arrived.

The whole time I had been speaking with him, Cook had a small caliber handgun in the pocket of his sweatshirt. The officers who pulled Cook over blamed themselves for not searching him, but I wasn't blaming anyone but myself.

I was lucky and I knew it.

For what seemed like an eternity I sat on that slab of concrete, alive by the grace of God. I could hear Richard Cook's blood run down the sidewalk and onto the street. Figment of my shattered imagination? Probably, but that is what I heard. Cops under extreme stress with their adrenaline surging, often hear and see things that seem almost unbelievable. At that moment, I wasn't sure where my mind was, but I knew where I didn't want my body to be; where it was!

Several minutes later the world began to come back into focus for me. I drafted another search warrant for Cook's truck, and returned to the house where the case started. When I finally made it home, I couldn't sleep. The incident replayed itself again and again, frame by frame, in my head. I am convinced to this day that if I had been an asshole to Richard Cook he would have turned the gun on me. I showed him a morsel of respect when he least deserved it, yet when he needed it most.

I didn't know it at the time, but the Richard Cook case would change my life considerably. Two weeks after this brush with death, I felt nauseous all the time and couldn't keep my food down. I lost 15 pounds in no time, and then called my doctor. I'm pretty thin as it is, and I didn't want a stiff breeze to blow me away.

My doctor asked simple questions. Did I internalize stress?

Did I let things bother me?

No way, I answered, lying through my teeth.

She politely told me that close to 20 years of pushing hard and the stress of police work were catching up with me. The stress needed to come out somehow, and unfortunately mine was coming through my stomach.

What bothered me the most was the plain realization of my own mortality.

When I strutted up to Richard Cook that morning in July, I felt invincible. The sound of that gunshot echoed for a long time in my mind and forced me to stare straight at a cold, hard truth. I'm not going to live forever.

I can still see Cook's head resting on the edge of the sidewalk and his feet pointed toward one of the old buildings that make up downtown Portland. And I can still hear the sound of the fireman's hose, as I was walking to my car, rinsing Cook's blood off the street and down the drain.

Chapter Nineteen

Hit and run

Aug. 25, 2004
Headline: DRUG AGENT INJURED AS DRIVER FLEES
Agent Erik Larsen was trying to question a man parked in a
hotel lot.

I have friends who are not police officers.

Some are construction workers, salesmen, lobstermen. But the only people who can really understand me are my colleagues in law enforcement, the people who see what I see and do what I do.

Police officers work side by side on a daily basis and, when necessary, we are willing to lay our own lives on the line for the officer standing next to us. We work together, play together and bleed together. Those bonds are tight. They give you comfort if you are ever hurt in the line of duty, because you know that there are a bunch of guys who have got your back.

Erik Larsen was basically a rookie when he was assigned to the Maine Drug Enforcement Agency in 2002. By that time, I had been an officer for 15 years, and a drug agent for two. When I was told that Erik would be working with me, I saw it as a great opportunity to pass along some of the knowledge I had gained. Now I'm not one to judge the looks of another man, but the ladies sure did like Erik Larsen. He was in his mid-20s and in excellent condition.

I guess you could say his workout regimen was a bit different than mine. He preferred running, lifting weights and riding a bike. I stuck to coffee and two-for-a-dollar honey buns.

Slowly, I introduced Erik to the dark side of the streets in greater Portland, where drug deals went down every day and every night. Erik was a quick study. It takes a special breed to be a good drug agent because you can't always think and act like a police officer. I taught him how to think five steps ahead while conducting an investigation. I gave him hints on how to interview addicts and dealers. I also impressed upon him my own feeling that to do our job was a privilege that should be taken seriously.

Erik looked even younger than his age, and by the time he grew his hair out and stopped shaving, he looked like one of the scruffiest shitbums in the area. We all have our strengths and weaknesses, and it didn't take long to figure out what he was good at.

In no time at all Erik was out making undercover drug purchases, buying crack and heroin while I monitored his conversations from my car. There was a calmness to his voice, telling me immediately that he had what it took. The reality is that one wrong word or move can get you killed as an undercover agent, but Erik seemed to take that all in stride.

As proud as I was of Erik as an agent, I was even more proud to call him a friend. That's why I still get pissed off when I think about the events of August 24, 2004.

That afternoon, Erik got a call from a woman who believed her son was in a hotel room using drugs with a well-known convict named Patrick Dorney. Dorney had a reputation as a thug who had racked up quite an impressive criminal record by the age of 26. He had been in and out of detention centers, jails and prisons since he was 13, for convictions that included drug trafficking and robbery.

I had never met Dorney, but I remembered his name and face from the crime bulletins shared by police agencies. The thing that always stuck in my mind about those photos of Dorney was his hairstyle. He reminded me of one of the Three Stooges with that bowl cut of his. Here's a guy who was covered head to toe in tattoos, enhancing his bad boy image, only to ruin it with a soup bowl haircut.

The woman who called Erik said her son and Dorney were at the Marriott Hotel on the west side of South Portland. I was driving around so I offered to stop by. I knew the manager there, a great guy who always helped us in the past. Mary Sauschuck, a Portland Police Officer, was riding along with me that day. She had been assigned to the MDEA for ten weeks, to get a taste of what we did.

I checked with the staff at the Marriott, but as I expected, Dorney wasn't there. The Marriott was way too nice for a guy with Dorney's tastes. The Amerisuites Hotel around the corner was a better bet. I told Erik and Kevin Cashman that Mary and I would meet them at the Amerisuites.

Dorney was supposedly driving a Mercury Sable, and all of us were on the lookout for that vehicle. Mary and I circled through the rear parking lot, and just when we thought we were out of luck, the Sable drives right past us into the lot. I couldn't miss that bowl cut for anything.

Now that we had located Dorney, we had to come up with a plan. The normal approach is to walk right up to the dealer and talk to them nicely. They usually admit they have drugs on them. Although Dorney had been around the block more than a few times, we decided to go with the simple approach. Erik and Kevin would walk through the hotel and out the back door. Mary and I would drive back around and come up behind Dorney. There were only a few cars in the lot, so I could see things pretty well.

Erik and Kevin came out the back door and started walking toward Dorney, who was still behind the wheel of the Sable, talking to a woman in the parking lot. What happened next was surreal. In real time, it probably only took a second or two. But in my mind it played out in super slow motion.

Just as Erik approached the Sable, Dorney stomped on the gas. Erik went flying onto and over the car like a rag doll. Dorney never slowed down and steered the Sable out of the parking lot and onto the main road.

Somehow, Erik had the presence of mind and agility to jump up in the split-second before the car hit him. That most likely saved his life. As it was, Erik had struck the windshield and rolled up and over the Sable.

I pulled my car up beside Erik.

"Are you all right?" I asked him.

"Yeah," he said, but I could tell he was hurting pretty bad. "Go catch that motherfucker."

My one overwhelming thought at that moment was to catch this prick that had nearly killed my partner. I gave the Intrepid all she had, and told Mary Sauschuck to hold on.

There was just one problem. In this race, I was outmatched. I had Dorney in my sights for a short time, but he drove like a madman and lost me. He got away. There is no simpler way to say it. Still, I knew that I was going to get Dorney, one way or another. I was not going to stop until we found him.

Amazingly, Erik had escaped the crash with a broken foot and some road rash. I guess you could say his physical conditioning program had worked. If it had been me in front of Dorney's Sable, they might still be scraping me up from the Amerisuites parking lot.

I focused on finding Dorney and putting together an airtight case against him, one that would allow the prosecutor to ask for a lengthy prison sentence.

Kevin Cashman took statements from witnesses while I searched the room Dorney had used. There was not a lot of evidence, but there was enough. There was a scale with cocaine residue under the mattress, and Dorney's clothes and porn collection were spread across the floor. All afternoon, officers from different agencies were calling my cell phone. They had heard about Erik and wanted to make sure he was all right.

At 7 p.m. I was turning over every rock I could find. I called all of my informants and put the word out on the streets that I was on a mission.

I tracked down one of Dorney's relatives, a guy who had helped me out in the past. Just before midnight I paid him a visit. He wasn't surprised to see me. I said what I had to say, and the guy told me that Dorney had ditched the Sable and was driving a different car. He was even able to provide a plate number. Even Dorney was smart enough to know that every cop in Maine was looking for the Sable.

After leaving the apartment, I had the police station put out an alert for agencies to be on the lookout for Dorney's new car.

Just then I saw a familiar face drive by. He turned around and pulled his car up next to mine. It was the chief of the South Portland Police Department, Ed Googins. He knew my whereabouts and said he wanted to be in the area, in case I needed help. His actions that night told me a lot about him as a chief and a man, and I'll never forget that he had my back when I needed it.

Within a few minutes, my information paid off. A state trooper was chasing Dorney at high speeds through the city of Westbrook. I was told that the trooper was Lucas Hare, a former South Portland officer and a good friend of Erik's.

The chase went on for several miles and ended when Dorney crashed on a side street, and got out and ran like the coward he is. I drove 20 minutes to the site of the crash, and by the time I arrived it was clear that Dorney had once again slipped through the cracks. I wasn't one bit upset. The plan was to keep the pressure on and to keep him running. Eventually, Dorney would run out of places to hide, or people willing to hide him.

The manhunt continued the next day as news of the incident made headlines in the local press and on television.

Scott Pelletier called me early that morning to tell me that he had located the Sable in Portland, up on a lift in a repair shop, smashed windshield and all. I went to the shop and started talking to the employees. This one employee in particular had an attitude, and was pissing me off. It was obvious that he was lying to me in front of his friends, so I looked at one of the uniformed officers who was there, and told him to arrest this asshole. I really had no reason to arrest him, but he didn't know that. I am allowed to detain a guy though, so I had him brought to the Portland Police Department.

The second that I walked into the interview room, this guy

starts apologizing. He said he was afraid of some of the people he worked with, and he didn't want to talk to me in front of them. The next thing I know, he tells me that Dorney is sleeping on his couch in Buxton, a small town about 20 minutes from Portland.

Right away I drafted a search warrant for the house in Buxton, and had it signed by a judge. It would allow the State Police tactical team to blow the doors off the place if they had to. By the time I got to Buxton it was dark and there were cops everywhere. Neighboring police departments were practically begging to help.

The state police were just about to enter the house when Scott Pelletier got another call. Dorney wasn't in the house. He was back in Westbrook and he was about to turn himself in to a Portland detective that he trusted. I'll always contend that it was not because Dorney thought it was the right thing to do; it was because we all kept the pressure on him and he had nowhere else to go.

I raced to Westbrook because I had one last thing to do. I had to interview Dorney and get some information from him that could be used against him in court.

In my mind, Dorney was a waste of flesh and he deserved to have very bad things happen to him. He tried to kill my partner, and he almost succeeded. It was probably a good thing that I had lost Dorney in traffic because there was little doubt that I would have rammed his car or done whatever I had to do to catch him.

Yes, police officers are human and we have the same emotions as anyone else. We're trained to control them, but there is a fine line in doing so. As an officer you can't lose your cool and do something that is unethical or illegal, but sometimes your anger is the only thing that keeps you going when you might otherwise give up. We all have deviant thoughts. The difference between those who go to jail and those who put them there, is those who act upon those thoughts.

An interview room is an entirely different story. Whatever

personal feelings I have go away instantly when I walk in to interview a suspect. It's like a switch in my head. I focus on what I need and how I'm going to get it. How else could I sit across from Dorney and not reach over and punch him in the head?

Dorney told me he didn't know Erik was a cop. Of course I knew that was bullshit, but I didn't care. I just wanted to keep him talking. I mentioned the few hundred dollars he had in his pocket when he turned himself in.

"That's probably not all drug money," I told him.

He took the bait.

Dorney told me that only a small amount of the money was from selling cocaine, and the rest was legitimate. That was all I needed, for him to admit that even $1 was from the sale of drugs. Interviews are like that. You give the suspect what he perceives as an out. He thinks he's outsmarting you, but he's really sealing his own fate.

Assistant Attorney General Lea-Anne Sutton, the best drug prosecutor in the state of Maine, took the case. Dorney was charged with four felonies, including aggravated assault, assault on a police officer and aggravated trafficking in drugs.

Sutton, as always, was masterful at the trial. The jury convicted Dorney on all counts. At sentencing, Sutton delivered an emotionally charged account of the events of August 24. I sat on the edge of my seat.

Dorney stood up and said he was sorry, but I just wasn't feeling the sincerity. I don't know if the judge did, either. I will admit that I got a bit choked up when the judge sentenced Dorney to 21 years in the Maine State Prison. Erik chose not to speak at the sentencing. He trusted the system and knew the judge would make the best decision.

As it turned out, this would not be Erik's only brush with death. He would be robbed at gunpoint by two drug dealers while conducting an undercover purchase of heroin.

A few years later Erik made the decision to leave the force and get a job in the private sector. I don't know all of the factors behind his choice, but I do know this: Erik Larsen was one of the finest drug agents I had the privilege of working with. Most of us take years before we excel at our chosen trades. Erik peaked far earlier than most of us, so he decided to try his hand at other things. He will be successful no matter what he does.

Dorney, on the other hand, is in prison where men are supposed to atone for their sins and rehabilitate themselves. For society's sake, let's hope he succeeds, too.

Chapter Twenty

The family tragedy of William Bruce

June 21, 2006
Headline: SON QUESTIONED IN DEATH OF WOMAN IN
CARATUNK
William Bruce surrenders to police outside his uncle's home in
South Portland on Tuesday night.

By early 2005 I was at the top of my game with the Maine Drug Enforcement Agency.

I wasn't *the* man, but I was one of the men who were called upon to deal with the cases that nobody else wanted or that nobody else could handle. For reasons that I still can't fully explain, I loved drug work and it loved me back.

But like all great runs, this one had to come to an end.

I knew what was coming when the South Portland Chief, Ed Googins, called me into his office. He told me in a matter-of-fact manner that my time with the agency was coming to an end. South Portland usually only loaned out its officers for a few years. I had been with the agency for more than five years, and South Portland needed me back.

The chief told me to wrap things up and prepare to come back to the patrol division. When I had gone to MDEA, Googins had said that would happen unless there was an opening in the detective bureau. Of course there wasn't.

So after five years of high-profile busts and constantly changing assignments that sent me around the state and beyond, I was suddenly back on patrol, right back where I had started nearly 20 years earlier. I immediately sank into depression.

I was lucky enough to get an acting sergeant's position due to a retirement, so at least I returned to uniform with stripes on my sleeve. I had to order new uniforms and a gun belt because it had been several years since I had worn either.

The toughest part was the shrinking landscape, patrolling a city that consisted of three square miles. My old friend Sean Lally best described the transition from drug work to patrol work: It's like going from 500 mph to stop in a heartbeat.

After a couple of months, I gradually accepted my role, and I was enjoying the challenge of relearning how to be a patrol officer. As a sergeant, I had the added challenge of learning how to supervise others. It's fair to say that there were occasions in which I excelled, and some in which I failed miserably. No doubt, the patrol division is the backbone of any police department. But I was, and remain to this day, an investigator. That is what I do.

Over the next several months I worked hard to find the detective sergeant a job, so he would retire and I could take his place. And that's exactly what happened in early 2006. Don't get me wrong; I didn't actually get the job for him. I simply told him about it, and he did the rest on his own.

Despite my not-so-perfect disciplinary record and the fact that I'm not best friends with everyone in the department, I got the job as the head of detectives for South Portland.

The role of supervisor came a lot easier for me in the detective bureau. I started to take great pleasure in mentoring. I certainly haven't done it all, nor do I know it all, but the experience I've gained from making hundreds of mistakes should be passed on. As far as I'm concerned, knowledge is wasted if it isn't shared with someone.

Shortly after my promotion I had yet another chance for a unique experience, one that I still share with younger officers.

When the phone rang on the night of June 20, 2006, I was standing in my kitchen, watching the lightning show outside, thanking God for a safe place to call home. The patrol sergeant told me that his officers had just arrested a man named William Bruce, who was wanted for questioning by the Maine State

Police.

"What do they want him for?" I asked.

"They think he murdered his mother this morning."

I was silent. It wasn't the response I expected.

The State Police investigate all suspected homicides in Maine, except the ones that happen within the city limits of Bangor and Portland. Those are the only two cities that have received the state's blessing to investigate their own homicides.

I called Abbe Chabot, one of the State Police detectives assigned to the case. I offered her whatever assistance I could provide, which at that point meant going to the station and heating up some coffee for her and any other troopers headed to South Portland.

Abbe told me that a woman named Amy Bruce had been killed with an axe, or a similar weapon, at her home in Caratunk, a rural community in the mountains more than two hours north of Portland. Abbe believed William killed his mother and then drove to South Portland, where his grandfather owned a condominium. That was where South Portland officers located and arrested the 25-year-old.

The lightning turned night into day as I drove the seven miles from my house to the South Portland Police Department. I assumed that I would be a cordial host for a few minutes, and then I'd be home before the 11 o'clock news.

Rain dripped off my head when I entered the side door of the station. I walked down the hallway to the two jail cells where people are kept temporarily.

William Bruce was wearing polo shirt and chinos. I did a double-take. He had a full head of wavy hair, and not one strand was out of place. To make sure I was looking at a suspected murderer, I confirmed William's identity with one of the arresting officers.

I had no intention of questioning William. That problem belonged with the State Police. But I did want to make sure he knew that someone would be speaking with him soon.

Through the bars of the cell, I looked at William and asked

him if he was all right.

Yes, he said, and he thanked me for checking on him. Under the circumstances, he was extremely calm. He had a fairly muscular build and it looked like he had just shaved. This guy didn't look like a killer, he looked like someone you would want your daughter to date.

Eventually some state troopers arrived and told me that some of William's relatives were insisting that he not be questioned. That was a decision for William alone to make. For the sake of caution, I decided to bring William to the Portland Police Department. Portland had recently installed a new recording system in their interview rooms. Should William consent to an interview, I wanted to make sure there was no question about the legality or the authenticity of the tape.

A patrol officer drove William to Portland, and I followed in my car. The State Police detectives still had not arrived, so I went into the interview room with William and sat with him for a few minutes. I knew that I couldn't ask him any questions about what had happened, so I tried to just shoot the breeze with him. I still didn't know anything about William or the murder, beyond the most basic facts that Abbe Chabot had shared with me over the phone.

I had been up since 5:30 that morning and I was getting tired. Lord knows I looked like shit in my ripped jeans and dirty t-shirt.

Once we got through the niceties of who I was and 'everything is going to be ok,' William caught me off guard.

"I began working for the CIA when I was 12," he said.

How the hell do you respond to something like that.

"That must be exciting work," I said. It was the best I could come up with at the moment.

I was realizing quickly that something wasn't quite right with William Bruce.

After a few minutes, I walked back out to the hallway to see what was taking so long. I was approached by Sgt. Anna Love of the State Police. We had never met before, but she was a dead ringer for her twin sister, who used to be a police officer in Portland.

Anna asked if I would sit in on the interview of William. For a guy who usually has a pretty quick comeback, I was speechless. I consider it an honor to be asked to assist another agency, but to be asked to help with the interview of a murder suspect was over the top for me. Anna said she had been watching us and felt that I had developed a rapport with William. Aside from that, she wasn't sure how William would respond to a female, if in fact he had just killed his mother.

Detective Adam Kelley would do the interview, as well. Adam was a towering figure in a fancy suit with spit-shined shoes. Our introduction was brief. Adam told me that he also had been watching my interaction with William, and he thought I was the suspect. We both got a chuckle out of that.

"Let's see what happens," Adam said before we went in to interview William.

I had done hundreds of interviews by that point in my career, and I wasn't nervous. But the thought did cross my mind that I could really mess this up for the State Police, or I could give them a big-time assist in a murder case.

For the other officers monitoring the interview in another room, Adam and I must have looked like quite the odd couple. He was a picture of elegance and I was a dirty former drug agent who spoke plain English, no apologies.

The key to any interview is getting past Miranda, and this went off without a hitch around 10 p.m. Adam did most of the talking at that point, and I just sat there listening for anything that would give us an advantage later on. Being second chair in an interview can be just as difficult as asking the questions.

William not only wanted to talk to us, he obviously enjoyed it. He seemed to find an intellectual challenge in having this exchange with two seasoned detectives. He was thoughtful and methodical in his answers.

I felt that he truly believed the things he told us – that he was a CIA operative with extensive military training, and the world was conspiring against him.

Two hours into the interview, I knew that William had killed his mother. Adam had finally told William that his mother was dead.

"Really?" was William's simple response. He had an eerie look on his face, and he never even asked how she died. He didn't have to ask because he knew.

The interview dragged on into the early morning hours. For an odd couple that had just met, Adam and I worked seamlessly. He knew when I had to interject something into the conversation, and I kept my mouth shut when I sensed that Adam was close to getting an admission. Every now and then one of us would leave the room and meet with the other detectives who were working nonstop to get more information. Little by little, the puzzle pieces were coming together.

William was indeed seriously mentally ill. He had paranoid schizophrenia, and he had spent some time in a psychiatric hospital. In fact, William had just been released from the hospital about two months earlier, and his parents took him in, despite the concerns of William's father. In the past, William had attempted suicide and had attacked both of his siblings, breaking bones on one occasion. There were other incidents, too, including threats by William to kill his friends with an assault rifle.

Dealing with emotionally disturbed people is one of the tougher challenges that police officers face on a regular basis. Mental illness does not discriminate. I have dealt with ill people who are wealthy and surrounded by loving family members and the best doctors money can buy; I have dealt with ill people who have nothing but the shirts on their backs and the streets they sleep on.

Men, women and children suffering from schizophrenia, bipolar disorder or panic disorder live in worlds that many of us cannot begin to comprehend, especially when those people refuse treatment or forget to take medications.

The system had failed William miserably. When he refused to take his medication in the hospital, officials there simply said he was all right and sent him on his way or perhaps they just couldn't keep him there legally. His mother had tried desperately to get William help, but it just wasn't there when she needed it.

During the interview, William never got upset and he never said he wanted the interview to end. We let him have smoke breaks, and we fed him the finest foods available to law enforcement officers.

There were several times when I felt he was close, but when a confession was on the tip of his tongue, he would slip back into talk about terrorists and the CIA training.

Around 10:30 a.m. on June 21st – more than 12 hours after the interview started – the state prosecutor in charge told us to wrap it up. Enough evidence had been gathered in Caratunk and at the condominium in South Portland to arrest William and charge him with murder.

I gave William one final shot to come clean. I went back into the room and told him he was no soldier. I was stern and looked him in the eyes. A real soldier would accept responsibility for what had happened. It was the first time I had taken a tone of accusation with William. He immediately said he wouldn't answer any more questions without a lawyer. This was the smartest thing he had said to me all night.

Adam Kelley and I brought William to the jail around 4:30 p.m. He thanked us for talking with him and for treating him fairly. We told him we would see him soon, and then we left him to fend for himself in an environment that he was ill-equipped to confront. Fortunately for us, prosecutors did not need a video recording of our interview with William, because Portland's state-of-the-art recording system had failed miserably. None of it was recorded.

When I finally arrived home that evening I was mentally exhausted. Usually I have a habit of running interviews through my head again and again. That didn't happen with the William Bruce interview. I was so tired I don't remember actually going to sleep, and I didn't wake up for 13 hours.

A Superior Court judge ruled that William was mentally

incompetent, and not fit to stand trial. He was sent to the state psychiatric hospital in Augusta – the same place where he had been treated and discharged before the killing.

I can't help but wonder what William went through emotionally when he was properly medicated, when the reality of what he had done set in. How does a sane person live with the fact that he killed his own mother?

To this day, William Bruce is living in a place where he is forced to take the medicines that make him act better, but probably make him feel much worse.

Chapter Twenty One

Sorting out a senseless crime

Every ending brings about a new beginning.

I had finally obtained the confession of Thong Nguyen, one of the robbers who had terrorized Alex and Julie, and in the spring of 1999 I was learning how hard federal prosecutors have to work to prepare a conspiracy case.

A grand jury indicted Thong on May 12, and the U.S. Marshals flew him from prison in Georgia to a holding cell in Maine.

Jon Chapman, the prosecutor who trusted me to solve the crime in the first place, and whom I now trusted to take it to the finish line, interviewed Thong with me after the court appointed a lawyer to defend him.

Thong's story was consistent with what he told me in Atlanta, and he provided more pieces of the puzzle. Three men – Dung Tran, Cong Nguyen and Quyea Le – had arrived at Thong's house in Georgia and asked him to come with them to North Carolina, to pay a visit to Kieu Minh Nguyen.

Kieu and his girlfriend Paula had recently moved back to the south from Maine, where they had worked at the Tran nail salon. Rithy, Paula's younger brother, also was staying with Kieu and Paula.

I'm sure Kieu's house was hopping around this time because Jessica and Alicia, the vivacious teenagers from Scarborough, Maine, were visiting. Also, another old friend of Kieu's was there, Nam Nguyen.

I can't say that I found the group too ambitious. The men arrived at Kieu's house and spent a few days sitting around and drinking. Then Kieu finally got down to business. He asked

Thong if he and some of the other men would travel to Maine and steal money from the Trans. Kieu laid out the bait. He said that the Trans had a bunch of cash, maybe $20,000 or $30,000 in a bag that Monica Tran kept in a closet in the family's apartment.

The plan was simple. Rithy would show them the apartment, and Thong, Cong, Nam and Quyea would do the robbery. Assembled over a case of cheap beer, the team agreed on a mission to drive to Maine, steal Don and Monica's hard-earned cash and bring it back to North Carolina.

And that's exactly what they did. But there were two major problems that these misfits did not foresee. They did not expect to find little Alex and Julie in the apartment when they arrived. And that bag full of cash? It was with Monica in the salon, and it didn't have anywhere near the amount of money that Kieu said was in it. At any given time, Monica carried a maximum of $800 or $1000 in the bag.

Not wanting to leave empty handed, the robbers took some jewelry and other items from the apartment, and hawked them in New York City that night. Hell, they needed the money at that point because they needed to get back to North Carolina.

I had spent months thinking that I was dealing with a well organized crime ring that specialized in home invasions, only to discover that I was looking for a group of not-so-bright malcontents. To think that they almost got away with it.

The federal grand jury process was slow and methodical. The great thing about it is that the witnesses are under oath as they testify, and every word is recorded and can be used in court later.

Thong cooperated fully and testified before the grand jury on April 28, 1999. His testimony, combined with the other evidence we had in hand, was enough to get arrest warrants for the other robbers – Cong Nguyen, Quyea Le and Nam Nguyen. Cong and Quyea were quickly picked up by a fugitive task force in the Atlanta area. Nam had apparently seen the writing on the wall; he had taken off and was nowhere to be found.

Cong and Quyea realized the situation they were in, so like Thong they admitted their guilt and agreed to testify before the grand jury. It was their best chance to get leniency from prosecutors and a favorable sentence from the judge. The federal system usually rewards defendants who cooperate, and really stings the ones who do not.

For us, all of the grand jury testimony was pointing in one direction, toward the man who was responsible for planning the robbery, Kieu Minh Nguyen.

Don and Monica Tran had given Paula and Kieu money to keep them on their feet and help them start their own salon in North Carolina. A few short months later, Kieu repaid the Trans for their kindness by sending a crew of thugs to steal from them. Now that's loyalty at its finest. The plan went wrong, really wrong, and two little girls suffered immensely as a result. Kieu was the guy I wanted, and he was the guy I would soon get.

The grand jury rose on September 29, 1999, and an arrest warrant was issued for Kieu Minh Nguyen. The charges were Conspiracy to Interfere with Commerce, and Carrying a Firearm During the Commission of a Crime of Violence. Kieu was not part of the group that came to Maine, but his actions set the plan into motion. The firearm charge was made because Kieu knew that a gun was going to be used in the commission of the robbery, so he was legally responsible for that as well.

Kieu was arrested in North Carolina and was flown to Maine. The other defendants had already taken advantage of the offers to cooperate, so Kieu was out of luck. As the saying goes in the federal system, "first in, first out." Kieu was staring at a long prison sentence no matter if he simply pleaded guilty or took his chances at trial.

The wheels of justice do move slowly, and it was February of 2000 by the time Kieu's trial opened.

Through all of this time I had remained in pretty much daily contact with the Trans. We had a bond that was unparalleled in my law enforcement career. They trusted me and I trusted them. Even when Kieu became a suspect, I asked them to let me do my job and not take matters into their own hands. They did exactly that. I learned more about patience and resilience from this family than any other I had ever dealt with.

Teachers aren't supposed to have favorite students, but they do. Cops aren't supposed to favor one victim over another, but the Trans were special to me. I knew them well enough to understand that a guilty verdict would go a long way toward healing their wounds.

My job was almost done. I had taken the case further than I thought I could, and for the most part it was now out of my hands. My role was to investigate the case, gather evidence and present the prosecutor with a case that he could win. I felt that I had held up my end of the bargain, and the rest was up to Jon Chapman.

Chapter Twenty Two

Helping a fallen brother

Nov. 10, 2006
Headline: CITY MAN INDICTED IN GUN BATTLE
Terrel Dubois faces eight charges, including two attempted-murder counts, in a shootout with police.

"We've had an officer involved shooting."

Those are the last words you want to hear when you pick up the ringing phone.

But there was police dispatcher Dennis Healy, on the other end of the line on the night of Oct. 11, 2006, telling me that one of our own was down.

"Is the officer all right?" I asked.

He wasn't sure. It was Steve Connors who got shot. My heart skipped a few beats when I heard that. Steve was a good friend of mine.

I didn't ask Dennis anymore questions, just told him I was on my way from my house to the crime scene, an apartment complex near the Casco Bay Bridge that links Portland with South Portland.

Emotions are funny things, rearing their ugly heads every now and then. I've always tried to keep mine in check, and that may be one of the reasons my stomach is such a mess. I can laugh with the best of them, but I generally don't have an outlet for the things that make me sad or scared. Those are the emotions that get buried.

So I was having quite a hard time with the information Dennis had given me. The thought of Steve getting shot sickened me. I had no idea if he was dead or alive. I was terrified, and at the same time I felt the rage well up inside me. Rage for whoever pointed a gun at Steve and pulled the trigger. But I had to control my emotions, because when I arrived at the scene I'd probably be in charge.

By that point in time I had left the Maine Drug Enforcement Agency and had been promoted to Detective Sergeant for South Portland, heading up the detective division. A leader must display confidence and determination, and that was what I intended to do that night. Any hint of indecision or lack of leadership would be unacceptable.

Driving like a madman in my car, I made calls to all the other South Portland detectives, and anyone else I thought might be helpful. Then I called Dennis back. He said Steve had been shot four times, but Dennis still did not have a condition yet.

Steve's nickname was the "Donkey" because of his stubbornness, so I was hopeful that he would find a way to pull through. My hope dimmed when Dennis added one more detail – one of the shots was to the head.

I made one stop at the police station, where I immediately received a most welcome update. Although he had been shot four times, Steve was going to be all right. Only the Donkey, I thought. With that load off my mind, I was ready to get to work.

A steady rain fell, and there were cops, bystanders and news reporters everywhere when I arrived at 204 Elm St. around 8 p.m.

Steve was at the apartment complex searching for a wanted man. It was a warrant out of the city of Portland, so three of their officers were with Steve. The police radio had gone wild when the report of an officer down went out. Cops from all over southern Maine started showing up at the scene to see if they could help.

We've all heard the expression that cops take care of each other, and on this particular evening this phenomenon happened like I'd never seen it before. Toss in pride to the long list of emotions running through my mind and heart that night.

I met with the high ranking officials from my own department, as well as the brass from the Portland Police Department. One of our officers had been shot, and three of their officers had been involved. At first, we got word that the suspect who had shot Steve had died at the hospital in Portland. That was good news for me, because it would mean the state Attorney General's Office would take over the scene. That office takes the lead whenever an officer uses deadly force in the line of duty.

When there is so much emotion involved, sometimes it can be best to step back and let a cooperating agency handle the bulk of the leg-work.

But if the suspect was not dead, that meant that South Portland still owned the crime scene. Over the next 30 minutes or so, we kept getting conflicting reports about the suspect's condition. So was this guy dead or alive?

Finally I had one of my detectives go to the hospital and get me a definitive answer. Indeed, the suspect was still alive. I mustered all of my strength, shifted into high gear and pushed all the emotions aside. It was my scene to oversee, and I had the right people doing the right things. We just had to carry out the mission.

I had Eric Jesseman, one of my detectives, draft a search warrant for the apartment. Not wanting to exclude Portland, because of their involvement in the case, I asked one of their detectives to help Jesseman. A judge signed a warrant and again it was a team effort as two evidence technicians worked with our tech, Mark Carlton, to process the scene and collect evidence. This was not a night to argue about jurisdiction or who should do what. The egos had to be left at the door.

The apartment was at the bottom of a set of stairs. I opened the door and walked into the living room, and I could see most of the apartment from there – the kitchen area, a bathroom and two small bedrooms at the back of the living room.

I don't tend to talk too much at a crime scene. I prefer to look at things and get a mental image of what might have happened. It sounds corny, but as an investigator it really works to put yourself in the shoes of someone who was there.

The actual shooting had taken place in the small room directly behind the living room. It was a bedroom that had been turned into what appeared to be an office. There was a computer at each end of the room, some paperwork on the floor, and two dog kennels on the far wall near the closet. Of course there were two dogs that had shit all over the place, probably as a result of the shooting.

I was surprised to see such a small amount of blood on the carpet, considering the number of rounds that had apparently been fired in there.

Steve Connors had been shot four times. One shot penetrated his scalp, bounced off his hard head, and exited a couple of inches from where it went in. Another round grazed his right shoulder. One pierced the left side of his chest and came back out, and the fourth round entered his left hand and lodged itself in one of his knuckles. While we were searching the apartment, doctors were extracting the bullet from Steve's hand.

We found some cocaine in the room where the shooting went down, so I called my old friend and MDEA agent, Erik Larsen. He came in and drafted another search warrant, allowing us to search for drugs.

Funny thing about those warrants, they only allow you to search for certain things, and if you take what you shouldn't take, the evidence won't be admissible in court. This investigation had to be done by the book and without any errors. Now was not the time to make an administrative mistake.

The adrenaline kept pumping through the night and into the early morning. I've been lucky that way. When I get locked onto something, my emotions block out the need to sleep or eat. I remain focused on the task at hand, and won't stop until it is done.

The rain kept pouring down as officers went in and out of the apartment, even searching in puddles for the bullets that came flying through the apartment. Despite the fact that he was shot four times and badly injured, Steve managed to draw his weapon and fire eight rounds back at his assailant, shooting him at least three times.

One of those rounds tore through his assailant's guts and that was why people assumed he was dead. He may have been knocking on death's door, but only the good die young.

The next morning, Erik Larsen and I went in to visit Steve at the hospital. I had to see him before I headed home to get a couple hours of sleep. He looked much better than I did at that point, but I knew Steve, and I figured he would want my reassurance.

Steve had been through some rough times at the department. I thought he would probably worry about the events leading up to the shooting, and he would want to know if it was what we call a "good" shooting, meaning appropriate for the circumstances and legally justified in the eyes of the justice system.

I felt I had a pretty good mental image of what had happened. Witnesses had been interviewed, evidence had been collected, and I had ample confidence to give Steve the thumbs up.

Ironically, he couldn't talk about the shooting at that point for legal reasons, but we really didn't need to talk much at all.

"Is everything good?" he asked.

I nodded.

"Yeah. Everything's good."

I could see his stress level drop immediately.

I left Steve in the capable hands of the pretty nurses and headed home. I needed to decompress and clear my head, if possible, before pushing forward. I needed to figure out why Steve Connors had been shot, and make sure I uncovered every piece of evidence that would send the asshole suspect to prison for a long, long time.

That suspect, it turned out, was Terrel Dubois, a 22-year-old player from New York City. He had been living in Maine for a couple of years, and judging from the evidence we found at the Elm Street apartment, his means of income was from cocaine sales. He had a warrant out for his arrest because he had basically kidnapped, threatened and assaulted his ex-girlfriend.

Portland Police had been looking for Dubois for a while, and he damn well knew that. In fact, earlier in the afternoon on the day of the shooting, Dubois called the Portland Police Department and spoke with a dispatcher. He made it pretty clear that he wasn't about to submit to an arrest. Any officers who came for him, Dubois threatened, were going to get shot up. That tough guy talk would also come back to bite him later.

Two days after the shooting, Dubois regained consciousness. I grabbed Eric Jesseman and off we went to conduct the first of what would be many interviews with him. Dubois looked like a typical trauma patient when we first met him at the Maine Medical Center. He had tubes down his throat and nose and he spoke with a gentle whisper.

Secretly I placed my digital recorder next to his head. His breath smelled horrible as I leaned so I could hear what he was saying. Just another example of taking one for the team.

Dubois was in the hospital for the better part of a month, and over the course of that time I interviewed him a total of five times. We established a bond, we were buddies, and we were tight; at least in his feeble mind. I was so nice to him it was sickening.

At one point I offered to get him a magazine to help him pass the time. Of course he wanted one, so I spent valuable time in the magazine section of a store trying to find the perfect reading material for him. It would suffice to say that his reading material and mine are not similar, but I did the best I could. Erik Larsen and I drove to the hospital to drop it off, and when we arrived the nurses were wheeling him out of his room to get a set of x-rays of his obliterated asshole. He picked his head up when he saw me and I told him that I got the magazine. A gentle smile came across his face.

"I love you man," he said.

I didn't return the gesture. It was fascinating that this guy actually thought I was his true-blue pal, after what he had done to Steve. When in reality, I was doing all I could to make sure he had a long miserable life in prison.

Prosecutor shopping is a big no-no in Cumberland County. You are supposed to call the District Attorney's Office and they decide who will be assigned what cases. To me this case was different, and it called for different measures.

Bud Ellis was a prosecutor who focused on felony cases, but he was also a kindred spirit. He enjoyed crude remarks, liked women immensely, and most importantly he was totally committed to his profession and he was good. I knew that he lived in South Portland because our sons would sometimes be at the hockey rink at the same time, or running at the same track meet.

I knew that if Bud got the case he would sink in his teeth and he wouldn't let go. Not long after the shooting I convinced Bud to take a walk through the apartment on Elm Street with me. That was the hook. You would have thought it was an episode of Law and Order the way we walked in together and started asking questions.

Bud had the mental image of what happened. Steve Connors had entered the apartment first, followed by Portland officer Bob Doherty. A woman named Sarah was there, and she went to a back room to tell Dubois the cops had arrived.

Dubois didn't come out. He waited until Steve and Bob rounded the corner from the living room. Then he opened fire, with Steve no more than three or four feet away. Falling to the ground, Steve pulled his gun and fired back. Bob also fired. Each officer hit their target, and as quickly as it had begun, the shooting stopped.

Dubois remained in jail while he was awaiting trial, except for his occasional trips to the hospital to get his internal organs fixed. All this on the dime of the state of course.

The trial opened on March 25, 2008. I had spent several hours with Bud Ellis and his trial assistant preparing the evidence and witnesses. I had confidence that we would win, and that Dubois would be found guilty. But I know from experience that you simply cannot predict a jury. All it takes is one person who doesn't get it, or feels bad for the defendant, and you've got a problem.

All of the officers who testified did a great job, as did the civilians who took the stand. Things weren't looking good for Dubois. I knew it was only going to get better because we all figured he had to testify. What a show that would be. Bud had done a masterful job and Dubois was the only one who could get up there and try to explain away all the damaging evidence and all of the terrible – but true – things people said about him.

His defense attorney, Neale Duffett, had been practicing in Portland for a long time and he had the respect of everybody in the courthouse, including the police. Duffett was known to be a fierce advocate for his clients, but he was also straightforward in his dealing with the police and prosecutors.

Duffett bought Dubois a simple suit at a local thrift shop, for him to wear to court. The lawyer did the best he could with what he had, but I always contended that he didn't have that much.

As the lead investigator, I was lucky enough to sit at the prosecution table with Bud, despite the fact that I would be a witness. Dubois didn't look over at me. I'm sure he felt betrayed. After all, I had been his buddy and here I was, throwing all of those interviews back in his face.

Those interviews did not even come into play until after Dubois took the stand and lied his ass off about everything that had happened. After Dubois dug a deep enough hole while answering questions from his own lawyer, Bud stood up and buried him.

Bud looked directly at Dubois and asked him if he recalled speaking with me on a specific date at the hospital, to which he replied, "No."

Bud almost appeared amused as he asked him if he recalled speaking to me at all while he was in the hospital. Of course, Dubois claimed that he did not. Bad move.

You can probably guess who the next witness was. That is correct, it was yours truly and I was ready to shine. At Bud's prompting, I slowly read several portions of the interview transcripts, from my little talks with Dubois in the hospital. In between readings I would glance at the jury to get the dramatic effect I was looking for.

The transcripts showed Dubois at his best: bragging of his drug dealing, talking about selling guns; displaying not even a hint of remorse as he said several times, "They might have been cops. Sarah said they might have been cops."

The whole point of Dubois' defense was that he did not know Steve and Bob were police officers, because they were in plain clothes when they went to arrest him. The badges and guns, and the fact that they said "Police," might have tipped him off, but we're talking about Terrel here.

Bud Ellis had a closing argument that hit every point that needed to be hit. I was proud to be sitting next to him when he finally thanked the jury for their service. The jury was out for almost an entire day before they came back with a verdict. Unfortunately for me, I couldn't be there when the foreman stood up and read it. My son had a field trip planned with his class at school, and I had agreed to chaperone. I've sacrificed many things for my career, but that day wasn't going to be one of them. I couldn't let my son down.

I was standing in the Museum of Science in Boston when I got the first text message telling me Dubois had been found guilty. You could hear me hollering over the noise in the electricity demonstration. I wanted to be with my fellow officers, but I was satisfied that I had been there for them when they needed me.

Dubois was convicted of attempted murder, elevated aggravated assault, and aggravated drug trafficking. He stood in front of the judge on July 7th to hear his fate: 35 years in prison. Should he survive that, he will still be on probation when he gets out, so if he screws up he'll be right back behind bars.

Amazingly, Steve was back on full duty within a few months of the shooting, despite the lasting injuries. He'll never be able to make a fist with his left hand. The doctors told him that arthritis would develop soon, and he would need more surgeries in the future on that hand. But true to his nickname, the "donkey" was not about to let one shootout put an end to his career in law enforcement.

When we talk about Steve Connors, inspirational is an understatement.

Chapter Twenty Three

System failure

"In a moment of decision the best thing you can do is the right thing to do. The worst thing you can do is nothing." - Theodore Roosevelt

Our criminal justice system is far from perfect, but it is the best one mankind has come up with so far.

It stresses fairness and proof beyond a reasonable doubt. It's no easy task to convict a person given the rights of a defendant in a criminal case. They are entitled to an attorney even if they can't afford one, and most can't. Defendants don't have to incriminate themselves, though most do. And those pulled into the system are entitled to a fair trial, not the kangaroo courts that are so common in other countries.

It's said that it is better to let 99 guilty people go free than to convict one innocent person. That's a premise I believe in, especially if I'm that one innocent man. On the other hand, you'd be dealing with at least 99 fairly pissed off crime victims under that scenario.

Despite the safeguards of the U.S. criminal justice system, mistakes happen.

In early 2009 greater Portland was seeing a string of armed robberies. Unlike bigger cities, when a place like Portland or South Portland experiences a rash of one particular type of crime, it is usually a single person or group that's responsible for most of them. This rash appeared to be no different. Most witnesses and victims described a white man with specific characteristics. The general description told investigators that the same man was probably on a roll and he wouldn't stop until he was caught.

For a while it seemed like the City of South Portland was immune from this robber. He was striking in most of our adjoining communities, but we were spared until Feb. 17, 2009.

I was at a training class, sitting next to Lt. Todd Bernard, when my phone rang that morning. We were making fun of all those officers who showed up at class wearing their guns, badges, and obligatory cop knives in their pockets.

Brian MacMaster was teaching this class and I enjoyed his teaching style, so I figured I'd give it a shot. Brian was in charge of the investigators working for the Attorney General's Office. We met the night that Steve Connors was shot and we hit it off right away. I took every opportunity to crap on him in a playful way, and he did the same to me.

I almost felt guilty when I had to get up in the middle of the class and walk out. Of course I convinced Todd Bernard he should come with me. What can I say, duty called.

Detective Frank Stepnick knew I was at training, so he tried to send me a text message on my cell phone. A typical text from Frank would go something like this: C@7sht bovbe. This obviously would mean very little to the average person and it meant even less to me. Frank investigated computer crimes, but he was out of his element with a cell phone.

I saved Frank any more embarrassment by calling him. He told me an armed man had tried to abduct a female driver in the parking lot of the Maine Mall. The suspect had jumped in the back seat of the woman's car and told her to drive. But this woman told him she wasn't going anywhere. I guess we all choose our battlegrounds, and this potential victim was making her stand on that morning.

The carjacker finally told her to leave the keys and get out. She ran like hell, hollering for help. As she was running she turned and got a good look at the suspect driving away.

As I was on my way to the mall area, things were happening fast. A BOLO (Be On the Lookout) was sent out to every police officer in the region. Within a few minutes, the woman's vehicle was located behind a motel on Main Street, only a couple miles away from the mall parking lot.

The officer who spotted the car walked into the lobby of the motel and there he was: a white male matching the description of our carjacker. Same blue hooded sweatshirt. Same jeans. Same work boots. This guy had the right color hair, the facial hair, and he was about the right age.

We all love it when a plan comes together.

By the time I arrived at the motel, two witnesses had already participated in a show-up, and they identified the guy as the person they saw stealing the car in the parking lot. If a suspect is detained shortly after a crime happens, police often bring the victim to the suspect for a visual, to determine if they have the perpetrator. The practice is known as a show-up.

I've never been a huge believer in eyewitness identifications. Officers make a big mistake if they put all their chips down on that gamble. Too often, the trauma of an event leaves the witness searching for someone to blame, and the sight of a person in handcuffs usually seals the deal.

Victims and other witnesses don't intend to punish an innocent person, but they want justice. I've seen a guilty man walk free because a witness couldn't identify them; and I've seen the wide eyes of innocent people when they have been pointed at, followed by, "That's him."

The man in the blue sweatshirt, Chris Johnson (name has been changed) was sitting in the back seat of a cruiser wearing handcuffs when I arrived. I took just a moment to open the door and introduce myself. He certainly didn't look like the vicious robber I expected to see.

Not long after I met Johnson, another officer drove a third witness through the parking lot. I asked Johnson to step from the cruiser as the witness gave him the once over.

Sure enough, I got the thumbs up from the officer. The third witness had positively identified our suspect as the carjacker. This was the beginning of a very long day for Chris Johnson.

The case seemed to be coming together like a 10-piece kids puzzle. We had three excellent witnesses who claimed Johnson was responsible; he matched the description of the suspect; and he was found in a motel lobby less than 100 yards from the stolen car. If only every case was this simple.

Everybody then went to the police station, where I was hoping that a confession would put any doubts to rest. This was my forte. The plan was simple. I would get Johnson to admit his transgressions, he would thank me, and off he'd go to jail.

The small interview room in the basement was typical, stale and nondescript. The only things to look at were white walls and bright fluorescent lights.

Johnson had no reservations about talking to me, and he was adamant that he didn't rob anyone or steal any cars.

Beginning with the second he got out of bed, Johnson gave me a list of everything he had done that morning. He seemed like a man who was down on his luck, but he was coherent and his story made sense. Although there was no solid alibi, Johnson didn't seem to have any motive to do what he was accused of.

I tend to dominate the conversation during interviews, but it was different with Johnson. I found myself wanting to listen to him. I wanted to read his body language. What was eating at me? I actually believed this guy.

It takes a desperate or vicious person to rob someone at gunpoint. Johnson didn't seem to be either of these. He seemed to be an extremely anxious person, but I saw no violence in his eyes. If this guy was lying to me, he was one of the best I had ever encountered. I seriously doubted that.

Because of the three witness statements, I told Johnson I had no choice but to take him to jail and charge him with robbery. But I told him one more piece of critical information.

"I'm going to spend the rest of the day following up every bit of information we have," I said.

"I'm going to work hard to prove you committed this crime. And I'm going to work just as hard to prove you didn't."

The process started with a timeline. I knew when the robbery happened, and I compared that with every detail Johnson remembered about his morning. I had detectives spread across the city to speak with anyone who had contact with Johnson. My gut told me he was in the wrong place at the wrong time, wearing the wrong clothes.

With all the information that rolled in over the next few hours, it was obvious that my gut was right. Chris Johnson could not have committed the crime unless he had a helicopter. He just didn't have enough time.

By 8 p.m. that night, yours truly had two major problems. I had to somehow get Johnson out of jail, and I had to start over to find the real robber.

For the first problem I turned to Bud Ellis, one of my favorite prosecutors with the Cumberland County District Attorney's Office. Usually we talked about how to get someone behind bars. It was an odd conversation when I told Bud that I needed to get someone *out* of jail.

I explained to Bud that we had probable cause to arrest Johnson, but it had evaporated during the afternoon. Probable cause is a standard used to determine if enough information exists to charge someone with a crime.

Bud passed the bar exam so I expected some brilliant legal solution to this little problem. What I got instead was, "Go ahead and get him out."

Bud had always been a beacon of light and this situation was no different.

I couldn't unring the bell and unarrest Johnson. He was already in jail and his bail had been set at several thousand dollars, which he had no hopes of posting. I had to somehow buck the system, because I was committed to ensuring that the system did not fail him.

With no small degree of pain I spoke with the bail commissioner. He understood my dilemma but his hands were tied by the laws as they were written. Chris Johnson was not going to spend the night in jail for a crime he didn't commit, I said, pleading with the bail commissioner for help in finding a solution.

The best we could come up with was for me to lie. I guess

sometimes the end does justify the means. I changed the booking sheet and charged Johnson with a misdemeanor theft instead of a felony robbery. That lowered his bail to $40 cash. The cash was simply the bail commissioner's fee for showing up and filling out paperwork.

Johnson, of course, had committed no theft, but this was the only way I could get him out. Then we would have the DA's office dismiss the charge.

Late that night I waited for Johnson at the jail, and when he walked out I gave him a ride back to the police station to get his vehicle.

I did most of the talking, and most of that was apologizing. While it would not give him his time or his dignity back for that one day, I told him that we did what we needed to do to protect the public. He was grateful for the efforts on his behalf, but I also think he was shell-shocked and just wanted to go home. I couldn't blame him for that.

As for the $40, I promised to pay him back, which I eventually did. This was a new one for me. I got more satisfaction from getting someone out of jail than I did putting someone in. Now I'm no radical do-gooder, but I certainly believe in doing the right thing. I look at problems as an opportunity to find a solution. Unorthodox as it may have been, a solution was found for Chris Johnson.

Within days of our carjacking, a suspect was arrested and charged with committing several robberies in the area. He could have been Johnson's brother. The real robber was ultimately sentenced to several years in federal prison. The only crime he committed but wasn't charged with was our carjacking. The feds wouldn't touch that one with a ten foot pole because we had arrested the wrong guy.

I don't blame the witnesses. Hell, I probably would have made the same identification if I was in their shoes. But you can't hang a case on a job half-done, and in our world the truth has a way of finding its way to the surface. It only needs a crack, and it's our job to keep searching for it.

Chapter Twenty Four

The body in the basement

April 20, 2009
Headline: POLICE INVESTIGATE SOUTH PORTLAND
SHOOTING DEATH
The news stuns neighbors, who describe Fred Wilson as a 'very congenial' man.

In every officer's career, there are those especially memorable cases that you never get out of your head.

You just don't expect two of them to start on the same night.

Somebody else took the night off on April 18, 2009, so I volunteered to pick up an overtime shift as the patrol supervisor. I enjoyed the pay. Civil servants quickly learn to take what they can get. I was hoping for a quiet shift because patrol was never my strong suit. I can do it, but I'm an investigator at heart.

Around 5 p.m. I was on my way to pick up something to eat when a robbery was called in from a pharmacy in the Millcreek area of the city, near the bridge that links South Portland with Portland.

As robberies go, it was as tame as they come. A guy had walked in and handed the pharmacy technician a note demanding specific drugs. I guess if you're going to commit a robbery you might as well get what you want.

This robber got his two bottles of pills and off he went to enjoy them. The pharmacy had pretty good surveillance footage, but there was one small problem. From the moment he walked in until the moment he left, the guy held his hand over his face. In our business, it's pretty tough to identify a hand. I took what I had for information – not a hell of a lot – back to the station.

I didn't even have time to sit down before the phone in my office started ringing. On my normal job as the detective sergeant I pretty much come and go as I please, but when you're working as patrol supervisor it's like the dispatchers have a computer chip on your forehead, tracking your every movement.

The dispatcher gave me a man's name and a phone number. The man wanted to report an accidental homicide.

Yup, that's right, an accidental homicide. What would you think if this happened to you? I guessed this anonymous caller was either a crazy person, or one of my friends looking to screw with me. My friends are really good at that.

I called the number I was given and James Pombriant answered right away. I told him who I was and I spent the next few minutes listening to him talk. The whole time I was trying to figure out who was actually messing with me, because Pombriant was telling me a story that nobody in their right mind would believe.

He and two gay friends had convened the night before at a home in South Portland, for a marathon session of alcohol, drugs, sex and debauchery, Pombriant calmly explained.

It had all gone terribly wrong, he said. His friend Bruce Lavallee-Davidson was using a gun in his sex play with the homeowner, Fred Wilson.

The gun went off and we would find Wilson's body in the basement of his home on Henry Street.

Pombriant was polite, sophisticated and he spoke in a manner that suggested an incredible amount of education. He almost sounded British. For one of the very few times in my life, I was speechless. If this was a hoax someone was getting me bigtime. And if it was real, well, I didn't even want to entertain that thought.

Pombriant told me he felt the shooting was accidental, but he didn't think it was right for Fred to be laying there. The shooting happened around 5:30 a.m. that morning. Pombriant said he thought about the incident all day, and he decided to call police after consulting with an attorney. By the time he spoke with me it was 7:30 p.m.

While I was still speaking with Pombriant, I asked two officers to come to my office. Ken Cronin and Jeff Pooler walked in and I put my phone on speaker. I finally asked Pombriant exactly where I would find Fred Wilson's body and he told me that it would be in "the dungeon."

He was kind enough to explain that the dungeon was a special room that Wilson had created in his basement, specifically for sex play.

Still thinking that I was in the midst of a practical joke, I ordered Ken and Jeff to take a drive out to Henry Street, a quiet neighborhood of well kept homes within a short walk of the Atlantic Ocean. Willard Beach is frequented by locals and some tourists alike, and you could literally throw a rock from Henry Street to the beach.

There were lights on inside the house and the front door was unlocked, just how Pombriant told me we would find it. That bothered me. I spoke to a neighbor who said he saw two cars at the house the prior evening, but he hadn't seen Fred all day. That bothered me more.

Nobody enjoys walking into these situations not knowing what you're going to find, so I decided to do what seemed fair. The order would be junior man, senior man, and then the invaluable supervisor would go last.

Jeff Pooler had several years on the department at that point, but he drew the short straw. Ken Cronin was closing in on retirement and he was going to nursing school, so I put him in front of me in case we needed his medical expertise.

The anticipation built as I checked out the interior of the house. The living room was immaculate with beautiful artwork and hardwood floors. I was impressed.

Jeff found the door that led to the basement and the descent began. One slow step at a time. We called out repeatedly, "police officers. Hello." No response. Another bad omen. Jeff made it to the bottom of the stairs and he looked to his left. Just before he turned his head he said "I have a bad feeling".

"I have feet," he said. Not what I wanted to hear.

Unfortunately, Jeff wasn't talking about his own feet.

Ken and I slowly rounded the corner and it was one of those *holy shit* moments. The black painted room was about 10-feet by 10-feet, with camouflage netting on the ceiling, rubber mats on the floor, and sexual equipment, tools, and toys everywhere in between.

I had seen a lot of things in my career, but nothing quite like this. And sure enough, right where Pombriant had said he would be, there in the middle of the floor was the dead man I presumed to be Fred Wilson.

He was covered with a blanket and only his head and boots were exposed. The strong smell of blood and leather were the only odors strong enough to surpass the smell of death in that room. We backed out of the room so we did not contaminate a crime scene.

We all stood there looking at each other. Then I had just one more thought. What if it really was the ultimate prank? I looked at Ken and told him that we had to go back inside. He was less than thrilled by that idea. But I wanted to be sure the person on the floor was a real person. How's that for paranoia? We went back in for a closer look. Suffice it to say, Fred Wilson was indeed dead, judging by the hole in his head. One bullet can do an amazing amount of damage. The point of entrance is generally much smaller than the exit wound.

I followed protocol and called the Maine State Police. Try explaining this situation to another cop. As phone calls were made between officers over the next couple of hours, the phrase, "you're not going to believe this," was heard more than a few times.

My night as patrol supervisor was over, and I was the detective supervisor once again. We discussed the importance of preventing any information leaks. This case had high-profile written all over. Sex, drugs, three gay men and a homicide in the Willard Beach neighborhood. All kinds of elements for the media to get their hands on.

The State Police came in and did their thing and processed the scene. I was grateful to work with one of their best detectives, Scott Harakles. I had worked with Scott before and I liked his investigative style and his personality. He is built like a bulldog, but he's an excellent communicator and a good guy. He seems to leave his ego at the door when he works with other agencies.

I was at Henry Street until 4 a.m. and was pretty tired when I finally got home. Things were in good hands and we had accomplished a lot already. We were fairly confident we knew who Bruce was after obtaining cell phone records, and Scott planned to travel two hours north the next morning to interview him in the small town of Skowhegan.

Around 6 a.m. my cell phone started ringing, and I was in a half-asleep stupor when I answered.

The man on the other end said his name was Bruce Lavallee-Davidson, and he got my number from Jim Pombriant. For the second time in less than 12 hours I heard the phrase, accidental homicide. Davidson said he was willing to speak with me, so I asked him to come to South Portland, and then I called Scott Harakles and gave him the good news that he didn't need to drive to Skowhegan.

Scott and I interviewed Davidson together, and my head was spinning by the end of it.

Davidson told us about a crazy night of preplanned drinking, drugging, and sex at Fred Wilson's house. He said they used industrial cleaners as inhalants, and it was something that enhanced the sexual experience. This was news to me. Hell, I'm just happy to have sex and I never gave any thought to enhancement.

Then Davidson told us he brought some guns to the party. He said Wilson had a sexual fetish for them, a claim that would later be disputed by Wilson's family and friends. Davidson said in the morning, just before dawn, Wilson suggested they play Russian roulette. Davidson said he thought the gun was unloaded.

Exactly what was said, and exactly what happened in those few minutes was only known to Bruce Davidson and Fred

Wilson, and one of them was no longer alive. The thing we did know was that Wilson – a hardworking, well respected brother, co-worker and friend – was dead because Davidson placed a gun to his head and pulled the trigger. Not once, but twice. The first time he heard a click; the second time a gunshot.

My prediction early on became a reality when Davidson was indicted on a charge of manslaughter. We heard prosecutors offered Davidson a recommendation for a four-year prison sentence if he would plead guilty, but he turned it down and the case was destined for trial. Davidson had AIDS and he felt that any prison sentence would amount to a life sentence for him, so he wanted to take his chances in front of a jury.

I was the first witness called to the stand, and was basically asked to talk about what led to the discovery of the body, and to describe the scene at Wilson's house when we arrived. There were sordid details that I wouldn't want my mother's ears to hear, and if I hadn't been involved with the case I wouldn't have believed them myself. Some of the looks on the faces of those jurors were priceless.

The prosecutor, Assistant Attorney General Lisa Marchese, masterfully painted a picture for all the jurors to see. It wasn't about an alternative lifestyle that many don't understand, nor was it about gunplay that went terribly wrong. Fred Wilson's tragic and untimely death was the result of one man's decision to take mind-altering drugs, place a handgun to another man's temple, and pull the trigger. That, I think we all can agree, is the definition of recklessness.

The jury deliberated only for about 90 minutes before returning a verdict of guilty. Davidson was sentenced to 10 years at the Maine State Prison.

The best part about that case was the opportunity I had to spend time with Fred Wilson's sister, and many of his friends, who taught me about acceptance and understanding. Yes, Wilson had a private life that very few people knew about, and which might be considered shocking to some. But there was so much more to the man. His relatives and friends focused on his kindness, generosity and all the good that he had done in the world. They put the focus on how Wilson lived, not how he died.

I had pretty much forgotten about the pharmacy robbery that happened just before Jim Pombriant called me on the night of April 18th.

Two days later I got a call from a man I had arrested some years earlier. Apparently I treated him all right because he gave me the name of the guy who did the robbery. Ian Bonville. The informant even told me how many pills Bonville got away with.

I knew Ian and had dealt with him when he was just a kid. I hadn't seen him in years. I knew that he had been to prison and was just released recently. During the time when Ian was locked up, his mother died and I was the primary investigator. I walked through her shabby apartment and I remember seeing her, slumped over dead on the couch, and on the wall behind her a photograph of Ian hung proudly. Her demons had caught up with her and she had overdosed on drugs. Ian never really had a chance, but despite the unfairness that life tossed at him one thing was for sure: He always loved his mother.

Ian had an aunt who had tried to help him into adulthood. When I got the tip that Ian had robbed the pharmacy, I called her. I knew I was heading in the right direction when she asked what had taken me so long.

The aunt knew Ian had committed the crime, but she insisted that he needed to do the right thing and turn himself in.

I made her one promise and left the rest in her hands. If Ian turned himself in within 24 hours, I would make sure that robbery case wouldn't go federal. Ian knew he would be facing a 10-year-minimum in a prison outside of Maine if the feds charged him. The federal system is far less forgiving than the state court system, and people like Ian know that because they don't just dabble in the system, they live it. A convict can tell you the minute he'll be eligible to get out.

It wasn't long before I heard back from the aunt. Ian was going to come in the next day. That was good news for me, because all

I had was a hand over a face in a surveillance tape. I needed Ian to confess.

I wasn't completely shocked the next day when Ian called me and asked for a couple of extra hours. He decided that having sex with his girlfriend would be appropriate because he'd be going away for a few years. I understood his plight and suggested he take whatever time he needed.

Less than two hours later my phone rang again and Ian told me where to pick him up. I went by myself because I told him that I would. I had another detective parked way down the street just in case, but I wasn't worried. Ian came walking out, wearing a Boston Celtics shirt, and he smiled when he saw me.

Some would say what I did was reckless, but I call it necessary. I told Ian to hop in the car. I didn't handcuff him and I didn't treat him like a worthless criminal. I treated him like a man. What he did at the pharmacy was wrong, but I knew he was a junkie and he was desperate. He never wanted to hurt anyone.

On the way to the police department we talked about the old days and I knew he was ready to confess his sins to father Webster. We walked to the interview room in the basement and I told him that I was recording everything. There were no secrets between us at that point.

I read Ian his rights and he immediately admitted to committing the robbery. He told me about his addiction to heroin and how he had relapsed after years of sobriety. He robbed the pharmacy to get some pills that he knew would help him get off the heroin again. He told me how many pills he robbed and corroborated his confession, so my case was pretty much wrapped up.

Ian maintained that tough guy prison façade until I mentioned his mom. He never knew that I was at the scene after she died. I wanted him to know she didn't suffer. He began to cry and it was obvious that his heart had broken when he was in prison and he couldn't be there for his mother, he couldn't save her.

I asked him if he knew where his mother was buried. A cemetery just west of the city, on the outskirts of Portland, he said. I offered to bring him there to see her on the way to jail.

He couldn't believe I would do something like that for him. Such a small token of kindness, when one least expects it, always seems to go the farthest.

The only thing left was a discussion about a recommendation for Ian's sentence. He explained that he was on probation for prior burglaries and he would be looking at the full three years on a probation revocation, plus a sentence for the new charge. He wanted to go back to the state prison in Warren because that was where his friends were. He needed to be sentenced to at least five years to be sent there. It seemed to me that he had spent many hours thinking about this, and he wanted nothing more than to go back inside. It was the only home he knew; he felt protected and comfortable there.

Ian told me that if I could get him a sentence of seven years straight time, which means he just does his time and doesn't have probation when he gets out, he'd plead guilty in court the next day. That proposal seemed fair and I just needed to make sure it happened.

On the way to the jail, I brought Ian out to the cemetery and he cried by himself for a while at the grave. That meant so much to him and took so little from me.

I called my old friend, Assistant District Attorney Bud Ellis, later that evening and explained the situation. He also thought the seven years was fair, and I had to convince him that he could pull it off in court the next day. I told him his biggest asset would be Ian Bonville. Ian knew the system and if he decided to plead guilty he'd make it happen.

Bud called me after the court hearing and told me that he suggested six years instead of seven. Still a fair and appropriate sentence under the circumstances, he said.

I'm sure I violated a departmental policy or two as I handled that case, but I didn't break any laws. And I still believe I did what was right, and what was necessary. There was nothing phony about the compassion I showed Ian Bonville. It was real, and believe me there are many individuals who don't get that same treatment. We were adversaries who ended up playing on the same team for a few minutes. We both wanted the outcome that would be fair, and that would give Ian the best chance at a new start.

When I dropped him off at the jail, I wished him luck and told him to keep his head down. He walked over and gave me a big hug. At least on that day, I had done my job right.

Chapter Twenty Five

In the hands of the jury

I paced the marble hallways at the federal courthouse in Portland.

The butterflies were there but I couldn't show my emotions. February 28, 2000, the day I had been waiting for, had arrived and Jon Chapman was putting the finishing touches on his opening statement. Kieu Minh Nguyen was finally facing a jury of his peers. The witnesses had been prepared and interviewed countless times; there was nothing left to do but tell the story of what happened to Alex and Julie.

I love the atmosphere in a courtroom. The stale smell. The tense silence, interrupted by moments of raw emotion. The looks on the faces of the jurors as the prosecutor turns a perfect phrase, taking them one step closer toward the truth.

Unfortunately, I would witness none of it during this trial. There was no need for me to testify, because this was purely a conspiracy case. Alex would have to take the stand, as would Monica Tran. The core of the case rested with the testimony of Kieu's co-defendants. Thong, Cong and Quyea had already pleaded guilty to their charges, and they were hoping for breaks in their sentences by testifying against Kieu.

I spent the better part of a week sitting in a small conference room that was about the size of a bathroom. I never heard one witness testify and I couldn't be there for Alex when she was being cross-examined by Kieu's lawyer. I knew she would do great. I told her what to expect, and Jon had actually brought her into the courtroom before the trial started, to get her familiar with the place.

Like an injured hockey player, I sat on the sidelines, getting the occasional update on the game. Jon would tell me who was playing well and who needed to kick it into high gear. The role I was playing was frustrating, to say the least, but a team player sometimes has to swallow his pride and listen to the coach.

The trial was going well until the co-defendants began to testify. One by one they took the stand and told vastly different stories from the ones they had told the grand jury. They all denied that Kieu had any knowledge of the planned robbery.

Now I'm not suggesting that Thong, Cong and Quyea were threatened while they were in jail, but something or somebody convinced them to stray from the truth.

Thank God for the grand jury transcripts, and for Jon Chapman's patience and skill as a prosecutor. As each co-defendant made up a new story, Chapman would steer him back to the grand jury testimony.

"Isn't it true that you testified under oath before a federal grand jury that Kieu Minh Nguyen planned the robbery?" Chapman methodically asked the defendants.

He would read back the testimony, as Thong, Cong and Quyea looked dumbfounded and said something to the effect of, "I don't recall."

The jurors had to have wondered why all of these defendants said one thing, and now were changing their stories. Chapman was confident that the jury realized what was happening, and that he could wrap things up in his closing argument.

While I had suffered through the week, I was determined not to miss the closing arguments, and Jon allowed me to watch. The courtroom looked like a cathedral. I kept my mind busy looking at the artwork on the walls, where they met the high ceiling. I knew that it was almost over, and I prayed for a proper conclusion. Jon's voice was strong.

"When you boil this case down to its core, to its essence, what it's really about is that this man, Kieu Minh Nguyen, through his own words and actions, through his deeds and what he said to the other people involved in this case, he put into motion a series of events that resulted in four thugs brutalizing two innocent little girls."

"This scheme or this prank or whatever it is they thought it was, this ill-fated trip to Maine on June 22nd, into June 23rd, which resulted in two little girls being bound and gagged and robbed and their world literally coming down on them, began with him, began with Kieu Minh Nguyen."

I consistently joked around with Jon and told him that he couldn't get a complete sentence out, but he certainly came through in his closing argument that day. It was not only moving, it was precise and clear.

Jon took his seat and he was expressionless. I knew that this was not just another day at the office for him, but a good lawyer maintains his poker face until the game is over.

The case soon went to the jury, and it was time to wait.

Kieu needed to be found guilty on the conspiracy charge before the jury could even consider the second count against him, the firearm offense. Sometime after the jury began deliberating, the lawyers on both sides were called into the judge's chambers for a brief conference. The jury had a technical question about the law.

The look on Jon's face said it all when he came out of the meeting with the judge. The question from the jurors was about count two. That meant the jury had already decided on count one. Kieu would be found guilty.

I exchanged a little smile with Jon, nodded my head and didn't say a word. It was over.

When we all piled back into the courtroom after lunch on March 3, 2000, the reading of the actual verdict took only a few minutes. The jury found Kieu guilty on the conspiracy charge and not guilty on the firearms offense, which for me would just have been icing on the cake. We got what we came for.

I was beaming for the Tran family. They placed their trust in me and the criminal justice system, and this time it worked. The verdict reminded me why I loved my job. And it confirmed that this case was never about me, it was always about those two girls who deserved true justice.

Nearly two years earlier, I had knelt down beside Alex and made a promise. Finally, as the marshals escorted Kieu away in handcuffs, I could say that I kept it. It would never have been possible if the Trans hadn't trusted me, and officers from Maine to Atlanta hadn't helped me.

Chapter Twenty Six

Sentencing day

July 12, 2000
MAN SENTENCED IN S. PORTLAND HOME INVASION
A North Carolina man has been sentenced to nine years in
prison for masterminding the robbery of a South Portland
apartment during which two young girls were bound, gagged
and threatened at gunpoint.

All eyes were on little Alex Tran as she stood at the center of the quiet courtroom.

Judge Hornby sat behind his table. Everyone else – the lawyers and people in the gallery and the defendant, Kieu Minh Nguyen – waited for the girl to speak.

She held her head high, just as she had the first day that I met her.

"My name is Alex," she said softly.

"This is to Kieu and Paula. I trusted you two, and this is how you treat me. I feel scared when you robbed me. You should be ashamed of yourself. How you feel if I robbed you? (Paula was never charged and there were no indications she was involved in any way.)

"I hope you stay in jail for a long time. You hurt me."

Then she spoke to the judge.

"Thank you," she said.

It was July 10, 2000, and Nguyen was about to be sentenced for putting in motion the events leading to the robbery of the Trans, and a terrifying experience for Alex and her cousin Julie.

Monica Tran, Alex's mother and the owner of the nail salon, also stood and spoke to Judge Hornby.

Monica said she had not been able to sleep or eat much since the robbery. Worst of all, she said, was the fact that it was another native of Cambodia who committed the crime.

"As I stand here in front of you, I feel very ashamed. You probably wonder why, because the people that hurt my child and my family is also Asian American. You see, it puts us to shame, we are hurting our own kind."

Monica recalled her own horrible childhood. She had been tortured and her parents were enslaved by the dictator Pol Pot, whose Khmer Rouge regime is blamed for the deaths of about two million Cambodian people.

She told the judge that all she wanted in life was to give her daughter the childhood that she did not have. The robbery took away that sense of safety, Monica said.

"This is to Mr. Kieu Nguyen. As I laid in bed, I cry because what you did to my poor little girl is unforgivable. You might not be there; the thought of you involved will haunt me for the rest of my life and my little girl's life."

"This is just a mother's cry for her little girl. She wonder what pain her child will endure for her life. How does it feel to be duct taped, tied up, gagged, gun pointed at and left to be found who knows when?"

"You see, I feel my daughter's pain. It cuts so deep that I had to write this and let you know. I told myself to forget. Many months have gone by. The memory and pain won't let go."

Monica told Kieu that her heart ached for revenge against him, but she had to let the government do its job. She asked Hornby to impose the toughest possible penalty.

Nguyen continued to claim his innocence. He said that if he had gone to Maine with the group, no one would have been tied up or threatened. He said he thought of Julie and Alex as nieces, and he would never harm them. Maybe he should have thought of that before he dispatched an armed group of low-lifes to rob the people who had given him a job.

Before he handed down the sentence, Judge Hornby reprimanded Kieu Minh Nguyen for failing to take responsibility for his actions.

"The fact that you stayed at a distance in North Carolina does not make you any less responsible than the band of thugs that came up here, because you made it possible," Hornby said.

"Essentially what you did was to arrange for a bunch of thugs as I say to come hundreds of miles to rob others here, to interfere with a business here, a former employer of yours. You may not have foreseen all the consequences, but there were consequences. I've seen no suggestion that you accept responsibility for what took place here. And it is therefore appropriate that you serve a substantial amount of time in prison."

Hornby sentenced Nguyen to nine years and one month in prison, to be followed by three years of probation.

For their various roles in the crime, Cong Nguyen was sentenced to six years and seven months in federal prison; Quyea Le was sentenced to 21 months; Thong Nguyen was sentenced to two years.

Nam Viet Nguyen, the fourth robber who had been a fugitive from justice, was arrested in Nevada exactly one week after Kieu Minh Nguyen was sentenced. Nam pleaded guilty and was sentenced to six years and seven months in prison.

Epilogue

My role in bringing justice to the Trans was one of the most satisfying rewards in my career in law enforcement.

I kept in touch with the family. They moved down to North Carolina, where they opened up a nail salon. Monica and Don eventually divorced, and Alex stayed with her mom and worked at the shop as she became a teenager. Monica sent me photos from Alex's high school graduation. I knew that everything was going well when Monica said Alex was a typical teen: mouthy, on the cell phone all day, but still loving her mom and staying out of trouble.

As for me, I'm doing OK.

I'm still the detective sergeant at the South Portland Police Department, where I have the pleasure of overseeing a fine group of hard-working detectives.

As you can tell from my stories, I'm just a regular guy who has tried extremely hard to do the right thing, for the right people, for the right reasons.

This book has served as a source of therapy for me. Some of these stories would probably still be eating at my insides if I didn't get them out of me. Living within the cocoon of law enforcement takes its toll. You see things that most people don't, and you learn to conceal the emotions and to bury the pain.

I'm not the same man I was when I first donned that uniform in 1987. My perceptions have changed, my ideas have matured and my naivete is long gone. I am now a by-product of those heroes, hookers, junkies and thieves that have been so much a part of my life.

Like most people in my profession, I have been thrown into literally hundreds of cases that I could write about.

So why these? They struck a chord with me in different ways.

While I am not shackled by these experiences, I do believe they have shaped the person I am today.

I often think of Bill and Maggie. While I have always had a soft spot in my heart for the elderly, that love grew after my experience with them. Elderly people have paid their dues. They are entitled to their dignity, and they deserve to be protected.

Renardo Williams was that case that we all pray we will encounter while we're on the job. Drugs, money, guns, and a suspected murderer! That case taught me a lesson about that most basic of human emotions – pure unadulterated greed. For myself and the other officers involved, we enjoyed a fast, yet short ride.

William Bruce and Edward Hackett each took a life, but their stories were so different. Bruce was seriously mentally ill and he took the life of the one person who never gave up on him, his mother. Hackett was that rare breed who seemed to have no heart, no soul, and no remorse. He had a craving to kill and there was nobody who was going to stop him.

Most people read about killers in a book or newspaper. Imagine spending a considerable amount of time with someone like that, and using all of your skills to get inside his head. How do you walk away from him without wondering why he ended up like that, and you didn't?

All of the stories in this book have their special places in the back of my mind. They bring out my sense of humor, my cynicism and my hope, my belief that we all share things in common, no matter where you have been or what you have been through.

We all make promises to ourselves and to others throughout our lives. I promised myself that I would leave law enforcement if I ever woke up and realized that I just didn't enjoy it. I'm still here. I also promised myself that I would stay true to my core beliefs, despite the temptations I would inevitably face. I'd like to think I have done that. I still believe in some outdated words such as honesty, loyalty, integrity and service.

We all leave some sort of legacy when we're gone. How do

you want to be remembered? I'd be happy if someone said that I lived well, I lived hard, but most of all, that I *lived*.

Because if you're not living you're just waiting to die. I don't have time for that.